Tao & Longevity

Master Huai Chin Nan

Tao & Longevity

Mind-Body Transformation

An original discussion about meditation
and the cultivation of Tao

Translated by
Wen Kuan Chu, Ph.D

From the original Chinese by
Huai-Chin Nan

Edited by
Karen Allen, Ph.D.

WEISER BOOKS
Boston, MA/York Beach, ME

First published in 1984 by
Red Wheel/Weiser, LLC
York Beach, ME
With offices at
368 Congress Street
Boston, MA 02210
www.redwheelweiser.com

10 09 08 07 06 05 04
13 12 11 10 9   8   7

Library of Congress Catalog Card Number: 82-60164

ISBN 0-87728-542-X
MG

Cover illustration is an embroidery titled *Old Immortal of the South Pole,
Symbol of Longevity* by the family of Madam Han Hsi-meng, the wife of
Ku Schou-ch'ien, middle and late Ming dynasty. Used by kind permis-
sion of the National Palace Museum, Taipei, Taiwan, Republic of China.

Printed in the United States of America

The paper used in the publication meets the minimum requirements of
the American National Standard for Permanence of Paper for Printed
Library Materials Z39.48-1992(R1997).

Table of Contents

List of Illustrations

Translator's Preface

Since childhood I have been fascinated by the stories of immortals portrayed in Taoist books and teachings. I wondered how a person could become an immortal and achieve the godship. I read hundreds of Taoist books but always had a complex feeling of fascination, confusion and frustration whenever I finished reading. They seemed to be written in such a way that only the rare person could understand them. The standard excuse was that the heavenly secret should not be revealed. I could not tell which books were good and which were bad, and I did not know who, among these many authors, was a real immortal and who was a phony or a fake. So, I continued in search of Tao in the Taoist tradition by looking for a genuine teacher and, fortunately, I met *my* teacher in 1961. He is the author of this book.

In China, people usually meditate in order to achieve spiritual growth and to *enhance their health*. I have lived in the United States for many years. To my surprise, the ideas and methods of Western meditation practices are quite different from those of the Chinese. It seems to me that most Americans meditate solely for spiritual growth and seem to want to expand consciousness or develop esp. Almost no one in the United States has pointed out that meditation can improve a person's health and cure illness. Although spiritual healing is presently quite popular in America, Western methods are very different from those of the Chinese.

According to Taoist theories and meditation methods, the mind and body affect and condition each other. Cultivating the mind for spiritual growth should be accompanied by a "lifting of the body." But since none of the Taoist books describe how to do this, this book has been written—the first of its kind to appear in either Chinese or English. It describes the physiological reactions and phenomena initiated by meditation in step-by-step detail, and ignores the traditional Chinese practice of private instruction. Professor Nan analyzes the vague terms appearing in Taoist books which have remained obscure to the average student because the ancients were unwilling to reveal their symbolism and provide clear instructions.

I believe that anyone who is genuinely interested in meditation will benefit greatly from this book. Professor Nan does not confine his attention to mental and spiritual development alone, but clarifies the relationship between spiritual development and physical transformations in the body. He also discusses many principles of Zen, esoteric Buddhism, and Taoism, revealing the practical phenomena of interest to all serious students of meditation.

Wen Kuan Chu
Los Angeles, California
Sept. 1983

Introduction

One of the greatest of all human desires is the desire for immortality. Matters pertaining to the origins of the universe, the roots of life, spiritual transcendence, and cosmic consciousness have also been pursued with intense curiosity. A number of important religious concepts are based upon these two dispositions. For example, heaven, the Pure-Land of Buddha, Shangri-La, and the land of great immortals all suggest the possibility of spiritual cultivation beyond the realm of earthly desire.

Our curiosity about the nature of existence, an inclination to seek knowledge of the root origins of life, and a tendency to long for immortality stand at the foundation of some non-religious schools of thought. The yoga techniques practiced in the traditions of India, and the meditation methods practiced in the style of the ancients in China are different methods of cultivation, but they are based upon a single body of knowledge. For example, both recommend that a person begin to cultivate and refine body and spirit in the course of the present lifetime. Further, they both involve the practice of techniques that may enable a person to transcend the bounds of the material world, to attain eternal existence, and to unravel the mysteries of life. These teachings are, in some ways, very similar to religious teachings but these schools are not religions. Thus, one who decides to practice these techniques is neither required to abandon any of his religious beliefs nor required to posit and adhere to any additional beliefs in order to begin.

Since ancient times, a great many books about immortality have been written and carefully studied. But who is a real immortal? Since it sometimes seems unreasonable for one to expect to live a long life, it is not at all irrational to suspect that the theory of immortality is based upon a lie. This sort of suspicion is not merely a modern one. Some of the ancients apparently entertained very similar doubts. For example, Chi Kang, one of the seven wise men of the bamboo grove, developed a theory of regimen in which he attempted to rationally prove that immortality can be attained. Since Chi Kang lived and wrote during the Chin dynasty, it seems as if he must have developed his theory in an attempt to demonstrate the truth of the theory of immortality to men living at that time.

Chi Kang argued that following a regimen for attaining immortality is appropriate since the way of immortality enables one to transcend worldliness and attain Godship. Although we may not be able to either confirm or deny Chi Kang's assumption that it leads to spiritual transcendence, at the very least we cannot deny that following the way of immortality is extremely helpful. Since following a regimen of this sort proves to be of considerable assistance to those involved in the Chinese medical arts, as well as to those engaged in modern psycho-analysis, physical therapy, and holistic health practices, it is well worth promoting.

A theory which has been transmitted from one generation to another for thousands of years must surely have some validity. Although the theory of immortality may not be easy to understand, we are not therefore entitled to believe that it is merely nonsense. Instead, we should attempt to discover why this theory appears to be incomprehensible. There are a number of factors which contribute to our initial difficulty. First, although the ancients were not foolish, there are vast differences between the teaching methods they employed then and those we are accustomed to today. Second, the number of people who have investigated immortality in depth amounts to no more than a handful since this sort of research requires stupendous effort and an ability to work alone. Cultivating immortality is not as simple as a get-rich-quick scheme. Those who are dedicated to the regular practice of cultivating body and mind will benefit from its tremendous self-healing effects, while those who practice only in emergencies will not.

According to the theory of "root bone," those who wish to explore the mysteries and transcend the world should have a natural gift for learning immortality. During the Ch'ing dynasty, Chao I wrote the following poem: "I had difficulty writing poetry. When I was young, I thought it was because I was unrefined and had not yet perfected my skill. I was very old before I finally realized that this cannot be accomplished by hard work alone. Three tenths of it depends upon man's effort but the rest is up to heaven." Poetry is a small Tao in literature, but some of the hardships one must endure to attain it are described in Chao I's poem. It is very difficult to change one's temperament in a short time, and thus to gain all the wonderfulness of Tao.

I wish to thank my students for asking questions and posing problems about meditation throughout the years. I hope that this book may help to answer some questions and correct some undesirable meditation practices. I also hope to clarify some of the abstruse points and obscure concepts that appear in the *Tan Sutras* on immortality. Although the ancients may have been unwilling to reveal a straightforward and complete account, I hope this preliminary sketch of my research will not only be helpful to those interested in developing a regimen but that it will also be a first step for additional research into the ways of Taoism.

In this context, the expression "first step" is a careful choice of words and not used as a consequence of modesty. This book does not contain an in-depth analysis of the Taoist theory of immortality, but it describes some of the physiological and psychological transformations that naturally occur during the proper practice of meditation.

Taipei, 1973

About the Author

The author, Huai-Chin Nan, has sought the origin and solution of life and the universe since his youth. He has traveled all over China and Tibet in search of truth and has inherited the Dharma of Zen, Taoism and esoteric Buddhism. In order to cultivate and verify these teachings, he remained in seclusion in the Omei Mountains in the Szechwan Province for three years and then spent several years in the Lu Mountains of Chiang Hsi Province. He has spent half his life as a hermit; he has also taught philosophy in universities. His knowledge is manifold and his wisdom is bright. He has written many books on Zen, Buddhism, Taoism and Confucianism.

The Translator

Wen-Kuan Chu was educated in both East and West. He studied Confucianism, Buddhism, and Taoism in the Orient for many years. His interest in science led him to the United States where he earned a Ph.D. in soil science from the The University of California at Berkeley.

Dr. Chu devoted his life to scholarship and was well versed in both the wisdom of the ancients and modern scientific theories. During his lifetime he worked to integrate these two systems of knowledge because he believed this integration will lead to the perception of other dimensions and promote the development of a new human reality. Dr. Chu passed from this life on Christmas Eve, 1985, while warning others of an impending flood.

A Note on the Translation

The word *Zen* has been used throughout the text since it is a term familiar to most Western readers. It should be noted that *Zen* is actually a Japanese word and *Ch'an* is the correct Chinese translation. Readers should understand that the terms are interchangeable.

Part I
The Nature of Meditation

1

Longevity is Actually Possible

Many people have asked again and again, "Is longevity actually possible? Is immortality attainable?" When people ask such questions I sometimes inquire, "Have you ever really seen a man of longevity or immortality?" The answer is always that they have heard from someone that there is a person somewhere who has lived for several hundred years. They often mention Kuang Cheng Tze at Omei Mountain and Hsu Che at Ching Cheng Mountain, each of whom is still living after thousands of years. But absolutely no one ever claims he can invite one of these famous immortals to meet the people.

At other times when people ask such questions I inquire, "Do you think meditation itself is the cultivation of Tao?" "What is Tao?" "How can you cultivate?" and "Why do you want to cultivate Tao and meditation?" Almost five pair out of ten will respond that they wish to have longevity and avoid illness.

Many people are eager to know about meditation and the cultivation of Tao. They wish to know how to open up *ch'i* routes, the conception vessel, the governing vessel, and the eight extra meridians. People also wish to know about the three *ch'i* routes and the seven chakras in yoga and esoteric Buddhism. They usually forget the highest principles, or the basis of philosophical theory behind the cultivation of Tao and the opening of the *ch'i* routes for longevity. If someone cultivates Tao for personal longevity, it is the extreme manifestation of the selfishness in human nature.

If opening the *ch'i* route in the body is the fruit of Tao, then this Tao is still the crystal of materialism. Is Tao mind or matter? Most people don't think about this very deeply.

Does this mean that there is no possibility for longevity? No! No! At first we have to understand two important points. 1) Longevity consists of maintaining one's health, slowing down the aging process, living without illness and pain, and dying peacefully without bothering other people. 2) Immortality does not mean indefinite physical longevity; it indicates the eternal spiritual life. What do we mean by "the spiritual life" in this context? It is beyond mind and matter, and it is the primitive beginning of life.

The functions and phenomena of the spiritual life manifest themselves in the physical body and consciousness. Its nature is very complicated and will be discussed in later chapters. Since ancient times, the ultimate goal of all religions is the search for, and the return to, an eternal spiritual life. Because of differences in language and culture the meaning of "spiritual life" has been expressed in different ways.

If Tao can be cultivated, is longevity actually possible? I would dare to say that Tao can be cultivated and that longevity is possible. However, one must realize that this is not merely an earthly enterprise since it involves going beyond earthly things. If someone wishes both to satisfy his earthly desires and to achieve immortality, his efforts will be in vain.

There is the old story of a famous man in a very high government position who heard of a Taoist who had lived more than two hundred years and still looked young. When asked his secret the Taoist answered, "I never approached a woman." The official was disappointed, exclaiming, "Then what is the use of cultivating the Tao?"

In addition to sexual desire humans have other desires, one of them being the desire for immortality. Seeking immortality, although the highest human desire, forms the greatest obstacle to spiritual development. An ordinary person has to give up many fields of endeavor in order to specialize in one field. This is especially true when someone wants to become immortal.

The *Yin Fu Sutra* of Taoism says, "Terminate one motive for gain or profit and the effectiveness of an army can be increased ten times." Just as when an individual develops his sense of hearing if he has lost his sight, unless one can give up earthly desires it is not possible for him to achieve immortality.

2

Meditation

In the Chinese manner of speaking, meditation—Taoist and Confucian—consists in "quiet sitting." Although "quiet" is the principal method of meditation, there are about ninety-six postures whose fundamental purpose is to facilitate the attainment of "quiet."

Quiet and action are relative terms and in a broad sense indicate two opposite sides of physical phenomena in nature. On a small scale they indicate rest and movement—two opposite states of humans. Tao is not movement or quiet; movement and quiet are each functions of Tao. Tao is within a movement and within a quiet. In other words, Tao is within movement and quiet. Therefore, if one considers quiet to be Tao, the concept is incomplete.

Quiet is basic to taking care of the body and is the foundation of meditation. When taking care of the body, its health and longevity (the energy source of all life) are developed in a state of quiet. The growth of animals and plants is accomplished in the same way. Humans need rest after action.

Sleeping is one way to rest, and adequate rest continually regenerates one's life force.

Lao Tze appropriately said, "All things return to their own roots. Returning to roots is called quiet and is named the regeneration of life." Further, he says, "Quiet is the means to master the effects of excessive bustling about." In *The Great Learning*, one of the *Four Books*, it is stated. "When one knows how to stop thoughts, then there is concentration; concentrate, then one can 'attain quiet'; by means of quiet one can achieve peace; with peace one can attain wisdom; with wisdom one can gain Tao." The principles described in *The Clear Quiet Sutra* of Taoism are also derived from the observation and imitation of nature. In the later stage of Chinese Buddhism, *dhyana* is translated as quiet thinking.

Quiet is the greenhouse for cultivating the "pre-heaven" wisdom, or spiritual development. Mere knowledge is obtained from using the brain during "later-heaven" life. Wisdom (*prajna*) is attained in the state of quiet when one gains insight or is enlightened. In Buddhism, discipline, *samadhi*, and wisdom are the three ways to attain *anasrava*, or no drip, leak or flow. The Buddhist assumption is that *samadhi* is at the center and prepares one to achieve *prajna*.

Quiet is just quiet. Thus, if someone uses his mind to seek quiet, that is, applies methods to seek it, he disturbs the quiet with mental activity. In Zen Buddhism a teacher may say, "Your mind is busy right now, so go rest yourself." The ordinary mental and physical states are usually active states. These mental states include consciousness, thought, perception, sensation, emotion, etc., and they are incessant.

Consider physical states. One has all kinds of feelings at every moment: the circulation of the blood, the feelings of nerves, and inhalation and exhalation. Meditation, especially if one has some latent illness, will cause tingling, chills, fever or sensations of heat, congestion, swelling, numbness, itching, etc. These feelings are much stronger when one is in a state of quiet than when one is not. Like the tree that wants to be still when the wind won't stop, one's mind becomes more active when it wants to be quiet. Beginners, therefore, often find themselves with chaotic thoughts. Sometimes they are even more unstable, perplexed and annoyed than when they were not involved in meditation. Consequently, they might think they should not meditate. Or, being influenced by Chinese legends and chivalrous novels, which often mention generating powers through meditation, beginners are sometimes apprehensive of being led down dangerous paths. These fears actually arise from misunderstandings.

3
Mental and Physical Conditions During Meditation

There are many reasons why people want to meditate. Some meditate for health and long life and some for long life without aging. Others meditate as a means of cultivating Tao and caring for the body. There are mental and physical problems that arise during meditation. The mental problems will be discussed first.

The aim and purpose of meditation are believed to arise from the mind. The concept of mind covers the modern concepts brain, consciousness and thought. Although this mind purports to achieve quiet by meditation, its early efforts are constantly flooded with disquieting thoughts. This is true because people are not usually aware of their minds being constantly full of thoughts from morning until night and from birth to death, like a waterfall never ceasing to flow. However, when a person begins to meditate, as a result of the relatively quiet state that arises, he realizes the incessant and chaotic nature of his thoughts. This is actually the first effect of meditation.

When a glass of water is turbid no dust is observed in it. But if a clarifying agent is added when the water is still, the dust can be observed to precipitate to the bottom. This dust is not produced merely because the glass of water is in a state of quiet: it was there all the time. Only in this quiet state is the presence of dust discovered. Similarly, we do not usually see dust in a room unless sunshine suddenly passes through the windows, which enables us to see dust flying everywhere.

Although we observe the mind's "dust" in meditation, it is not necessary to remove it by any particular method. By just keeping quiet and not shaking or moving so as to neither increase nor decrease it, this mental dust will naturally stop flying around.

The second problem most likely to arise is that a person gets sleepy whenever he is in a relatively quiet condition and may fall asleep unwittingly. If this happens, he should carefully check himself to determine whether his sleepy condition is from physical or mental fatigue. If so, he should go to sleep immediately. After sufficient sleep, with vitality renewed, he should then meditate again. If he finds, however, that there is no fatigue in mind or body, it is better to get up to do a little exercise. The spirit thus roused, he will be able to maintain an appropriate and stable state of quietude.

4
Ch'i Phenomena of the Body

Ancient oriental medical science and witchcraft have the same origins; Chinese medicine is no exception. About three thousand years ago, during the Chou and Ch'in dynasties, the practitioners of the Chinese medical arts turned from witch-doctor practices and shamanism to the methods and technology of Taoism. Chinese medical science, the technology of Taoism, and the methods of Indian yoga all recognize that the source of human life is in the infinite storage of *ch'i*, the potential energy latent within the body. In ancient Taoist sutras the primitive character 炁 is used to represent *ch'i*. If we disassemble this character, 旡 the ancient character for 無 , meaning none. The 灬 has the same meaning as 火 , fire. In other words, *ch'i*, 炁 , means *no fire*. What is meant by fire? Sexual desires, lust-filled affections and attractions, restless, bustling thoughts and a reckless mind are all connoted by fire. In the absence of this rapidly burning and all consuming fire, one would be filled with vitality. In Chinese medicine, fire that is moving restlessly is called *secondary fire*, whereas fire in the correct position and proper condition is known as *ruling fire*. When one has ruling fire and is full of potential energy, the latent *ch'i* can then be induced.

The terms latent energy, kundalini, etc., are well known in yoga, esoteric Buddhism and Taoism. However, most who engage in these practices misunderstand the nature of this latent energy or kundalini, and therefore may die of high blood pressure, congestion in the brain, or senile psychoses such as schizophrenia. They do not know that the so-called kundalini is the warmth phenomenon of the heat *Dharma*, which in Buddhism is the first stage of *catus-kusala-mula* (the four good roots of spring fruit or the sources of development). It is easy to mistake the feeling of warmth or heat around the lower abdomen or perineum for the awakening of kundalini. This is often an evil fire, rather than a genuine awakening of the latent energy.

The ancient Chinese measured time by the movement of the sun and moon and they divided a day into twelve hours. Each Chinese hour is double, equivalent to two sixty-minute-hours. The twelve Chinese double hours correspond to the twelve meridians, *i.e.*, the channels through which vital energy flows in a living body. The practice of acupuncture is based upon the principle that *ch'i* (or vital energy) is flowing through a specific channel during each double hour.

The twelve meridians are important in medical science but there are additional *ch'i* routes, not included among these twelve, that are important in Taoism. This involves the *chi ching pa mai*, or the eight extra meridians, which are the *Tu Mai, Jen Mai, Ch'ong Mai, Tai Mai, Yang Wei, Yin Wei, Yang Ch'iao,* and *Yin Ch'iao.*

The *Chuang Tze* mentions the correspondences between the *Tu Mai* and the human body. The *Tu Mai* corresponds to the spinal cord of the central nervous system. *Jen Mai* corresponds to the autonomic nervous system and the visceral organs. *Tai Mai* corresponds to the kidney nervous system. *Yang Wei* and *Yin Wei* have a close relationship with the cerebrum, cerebellum, and diencephalon[1] nervous systems. *Yang Ch'iao* and *Yin Ch'iao* correspond to the genital nervous system, including the prostate gland and the nerve functions in the hands and feet. It is difficult to define *Ch'ong Mai* but we can say that it flows somewhere between the central and autonomic nervous systems, although it has no fixed position or range. It starts between the testes and the penis in a male and between the vagina and the uterus in a female. It rushes upward to pass through the stomach and the heart and then rushes toward the center of the head. Only a person who opens up some *ch'i* route and actually experiences the circulation of *ch'i* will be convinced that *ch'i* and *ch'i* channels are real.[2]

Tan Tien and Chakras

In esoteric Buddhism and Indian yoga, it is supposed that there are three *ch'i* routes and seven chakras. The three *ch'i* routes are the left, right and middle *ch'i* channels located in the

---

[1]Diencephalon is a modern term. The ancients did not know neuroanatomy and therefore this term shall not be used again. The reader will be referred to "the center of the head," or "the top of the head," which is actually a more correct translation of the material.

[2]I have not been trained in Western medicine and the medical terms used here in connection with *ch'i* are based upon knowledge acquired from experience and my own research.

torso. The seven chakras correspond to the major nerve plexus in the human body. In Taoism, on the other hand, it is supposed that there are front (*Jen Mai*), back (*Tu Mai*) and middle (*Ch'ong Mai*) *ch'i* routes in the torso. There is also the Taoist theory of upper *Tan Tien*, middle *Tan Tien* and lower *Tan Tien*. The *Tan Tien* and the chakras are different although they have similar functions and effects.

The upper *Tan Tien* is located in the center of the head, behind the point between the two eyebrows. The middle *Tan Tien* is located at a point bisecting the chest between the breasts. The lower *Tan Tien* is located approximately four fingers below the navel.[3]

Tan means the pill of immortality. *Tien* means a field. This does not, as is sometimes believed, indicate that one can devise a pill, an elixir, or decoction that will confer immortality inside the *Tan Tien*. If it were possible to create a pill of immortality inside *Tan Tien*, it would be a malignant growth rather than something beneficial.

The chakras in yoga are now regarded as major nerve plexuses. The important nerve plexuses from the center of the head to the perineum are believed to be *chakras*, but this is difficult to confirm. The fact is that the chakras and nerve plexuses are closely related.

Meditation and the Ch'i Route

During meditation one becomes mentally quieter, and thinking slows down or ceases. The circulation of the blood becomes slower, so the burden on the heart is decreased. When one meditates in a correct posture, not exhausting energy through action, the endocrine secretion of the pituitary gland is evenly distributed, gradually creating the feeling of being full of *ch'i*. The most noticeable sensations occur in the central nervous system, at the end of the spinal cord and in the kidneys, and one may feel tightness or swelling at these places. The *ch'i* gradually

---

[3]There is another Taoist point called *Chong Kung* (literally meaning, middle palace), which is located between the stomach and the diaphragm.

advances from these locations, creating a serpentine sensation as it moves through a *ch'i* route.

This describes what happens in the case of a normal, average person. However, if one has certain illnesses, or latent illnesses, or if one is much healthier and stronger than the ordinary person, things will be different. Everybody has different mental and physical conditions and will therefore notice different phenomena. One rule cannot be applied to all.

In seeking quiet during meditation, the mental and physical functions may be classified into two parts: consciousness and sensation, or feeling. Consciousness includes thoughts, images, etc. Feeling includes emotions, physical sensations and *ch'i* circulation. Both consciousness and sensation are actually motions of the mind.

When the *ch'i* starts to move, most people subconsciously focus on the feeling of *ch'i's* circulation, and it becomes much stronger. The movement of *ch'i* is then disturbed by one's mental force, causing deception, illusions, association of ideas, chaotic mental states, etc. Some might even frivolously suppose that they have already opened the *ch'i* route. Others, because of illusions caused by concentrated attention, tighten their nerves and fall into states of mental and physical sickness.

Meditation does not drive a man crazy. But, misunderstanding brought about by ignorance of the basic principles of meditation can cause abnormal mental states and disturb the quiet of meditation.

5

Postures in Meditation

Confucianism, Buddhism, and Taoism have handed down from ancient times ninety-six kinds of meditation postures, including some sleeping postures. The most popular posture in Buddhism is crossing the legs in the half-lotus or full-lotus.

The rationalists after the Sung dynasty started their own meditation methods, which were influenced by Buddhism and Taoism. Ch'eng Ming Tao promoted the idea that one should cultivate one's nature and metaphysics in quietude. His brother, Cheng I Ch'uan, added the method of "Chun Ching" (to cleanse the mind through a serious attitude). Confucianists have practiced meditation ever since, by simply sitting seriously on a chair with the hands on the knees.

Taoism uses the lotus and sleeping postures. Depending on physical demands and cultivation of the *ch'i* route, different postures are sometimes used.

The Lotus Postures

The lotus posture is also called the *seven branch sitting* method, because it involves seven key points of the body.

1) Cross both legs (lotus posture). If one cannot do this, then cross one leg, either with the right leg over the left leg, or with the left leg over the right leg. If one cannot even make a half-lotus, one can just cross the legs tailor fashion.

2) The head, neck, and spine must be kept vertically in a straight line. If one is weak or sick, do not try very hard to be absolutely straight.

3) Rest the right hand on the left hand, palms upward, with the tip of the thumbs touching, and rest them in the lap. This is called the *samadhi* seal.

4) Keep the shoulders erect without tension; do not let the shoulders droop or fall forward.

5) Straighten the head, pull back the chin to press the two (left and right) large arteries a slight bit.

6) Open the eyes slightly, seeing without looking. Fix your sight about seven to eight feet ahead or farther. For those who use their eyes a great deal it is better to close the eyes first in meditation.

7) Put your tongue to the salivary gland of the incisor gums. This is the way a baby who has no teeth sleeps.

Figure 5.1
Full-Lotus Posture

Additional Directions and Postures

1) Relax the body, brain and nerves. Also loosen the muscles so as not to be under any tension. Smile a little, because a person's nerves are at ease when smiling.

2) Beginners should not meditate too soon after meals, since this might cause indigestion. Also, do not meditate when you feel hungry; it might disturb your meditation.

3) Some ventilation is desirable, but one should not let the air blow directly on the body.

4) Do not meditate in a dark place; otherwise, you might tend to fall asleep. Do not meditate under bright lights either; you might tend to be under tension as a consequence.

Figure 5.2
Half-Lotus Posture

Right leg over left leg.   Left leg over right leg.

5) Beginners should not try to meditate too long; rather, meditate for only a short time and meditate more often.

6) A cushion should be used. Adjust the height individually. The rule is to be comfortable. Too high or too low a cushion can induce tension. The firmness of a cushion also has to be selected for comfort.

7) When the weather is cold, use a blanket to keep your knees and neck warm. Otherwise, you will be afflicted by a cold, and there is no medicine to cure that. This is important.

8) When you are finished with your meditation, you should use your palms to massage your face and feet before arising. It is also beneficial to do some suitable exercise after meditation.

If you cannot assume the half-lotus posture, or if you meditate in half-lotus until the feet go to sleep and want to continue meditating, change to one of the postures indicated in figures 5.3 through 5.10 on pages 16-18.

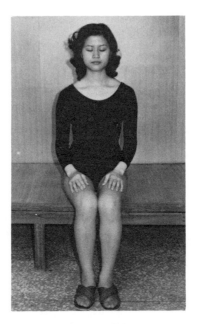

Figure 5.3
Sitting on a Chair Posture

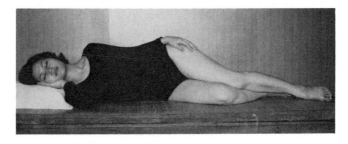

Figure 5.4
Sleeping Posture

Figure 5.5
Lion Posture

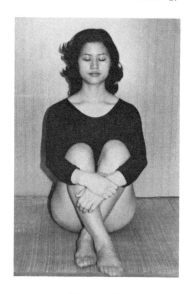

Figure 5.6
Immortal Posture

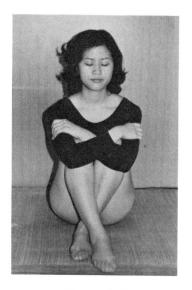

Figure 5.7
Six Furnace Posture

Figure 5.8
Bodhisattva Posture

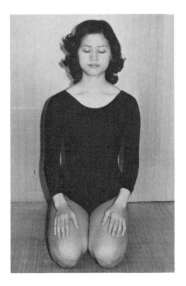

Figure 5.9
**Bestriding Crane
Posture (1)**

Figure 5.10
**Bestriding Crane
Posture (2)**

Hand Positions—Mudras or Signs

In general, the spinal cord is the center of the nervous system of the human body, with the nerves distributed to the left and right, and interlaced. They are somewhat like the branches of a tree, distributed along the central trunk.

The lotus (seven branch) posture crosses and interlaces the hands and feet. It has the effect of communicating the *ch'i* from left to right and from right to left, and then returning it to the center. In other words, the energy of the left side (yang) and the right side (yin) can communicate with each other. This therefore decreases the scattering of energy; each side has the function of adjusting the other and recovering the primitive vitality.

In this posture the hands and feet are also at rest, which decreases the burden on the heart. The function of the heart will therefore recover more the longer one meditates.

Effects on Health—The Head

In the lotus posture the head is in the proper position, the cerebrum is slightly backward so that the pituitary gland will not be pressed and will be able to recover its normal function. The uniform endocrine secretion of the pituitary gland will then recover the normal functions of the thyroid gland, lymph nodes, and adrenal glands. The chin is next pulled back a bit to put a slight pressure on the two large arteries. The pumping of the blood to the brain is therefore somewhat slowed down. This enables one to decrease nervous tension and the mad coursing of thought. It is also helpful for normalizing blood pressure.

Effects on Health—Crossed Legs

Some people fear that crossing the legs in meditation not only constitutes a hazard to health, but that the pressing of the blood vessels of the legs may lead to a serious illness such as phlebitis, etc. Therefore, a disagreeable tingling or numbness in the legs during meditation causes some people to become apprehensive. This is a misunderstanding. Actually, one's health has an important relationship with one's legs and feet. (For example, a toxic condition in the system might well be a contributing factor to phlebitis in the legs.) Ancient Chinese Taoist medical theory holds that "vitality is generated from the soles of the feet." This is very true. One's health and long life have a direct relation with the condition of his feet and legs. Babies and tiny tots move their feet and legs constantly. After middle age, one feels less strength beneath the waist and likes to raise the feet, e.g., when sitting. Deterioration and death usually originate in the feet and legs and gradually move upward to the trunk and head. If one's legs feel uncomfortable and numb and go to sleep during meditation in the crossed leg posture, it suggests that that one has latent health problems and indicates that the nerves and blood vessels in the legs are not in good condition. (See p. 37.)

After freeing the legs and waiting until the tingling and numbness have subsided or abated, one feels a kind of euphoria never before experienced. If you can persist in meditating until your *ch'i* and blood flow freely to the legs, you will have a strong internal orgasm from your feet and legs upward to your waist and back, and even throughout your entire body. Rest assured. You would then not want to release your legs and stop your meditation prematurely.

The human body can be compared to a tree. A tree sinks its crooked roots into the ground. With sunshine, air, and nutrition from the soil it keeps growing. Man, on the other hand, has his roots in his head. His soil is in space. Man's feet are like the branches of ginseng. Crossing the legs is therefore tantamount to bending the branches of ginseng or a pine tree whose crooked branches form into knots so that its growing force will not be scattered outside. It can thus return to its original source for cultivation and consequently become stronger.

Crossing the legs does not bother one's health. In fact, if one practices correctly, it will help his health and longevity.

6

Use of the Mind in Meditation

In general, seventy percent of those who learn meditation do so for health and for long life. For such purposes meditation need not be difficult. Twenty percent study meditation out of curiosity or because they are seeking something wonderful and subtle, such as clairvoyance or telepathy. The remaining ten percent are seeking the Tao. It is hard to find one person in ten thousand, even among those seeking Tao, who really understands the Tao and the right way to cultivate it. It is not easy to use the mind effectively in this quest.

A person should have a fairly clear idea of what he hopes to accomplish by engaging in meditation before he begins. There are a great many different meditation techniques and one should practice a method that will enable him to achieve the sort of mental cultivation he desires. In China, the most popular methods of cultivation are those derived from Buddhism and Taoism but there are also many methods that were not derived from either one of these two traditions.[4]

The most popular Buddhist methods are reciting the names of Buddha, cultivating *Chih* and *Kuan* (*i.e.*, quiet sitting and contemplation), observing the mind, or employing Zen techniques. For those who truly believe in the esoteric teachings, incantations, chanting mantras or visualization methods are regarded as ideal. Those who employ Buddhist meditation methods generally suppose mental cultivation is sufficient. As a consequence, physical transformations and bodily changes are ignored.

Taoist meditation methods, on the other hand, place great emphasis on physical changes. They even consider opening the *Tu Mai, Jen Mai* and all eight extra meridians, recovering health, and increasing a person's allotted lifespan as the natural effect of Tao. If one knows how to cultivate only the mind by means of Buddhist methods and does not know the wonders of physical change, his cultivation is not consistent with Tao. Taoists therefore criticize Buddhist methods as showing only "the cultivation of their nature," and not "the cultivation of life." Taoists consequently insist that "cultivation of both nature and

---

[4]It is not possible, in this context, to distinguish between Buddhist and Taoist meditation techniques. Further, although there are both correct and incorrect methods of mental cultivation, it is not possible to categorize them here.

life" is the genuine Tao and believe that the cultivation of life without the cultivation of nature is a major mistake. It has been said that "By cultivation of nature only, without the cultivation of life, the yin spirit will not become a saint in ten thousand kalpas." In his commentary on *I Ching*, Confucius says that we should "Probe the principle to the depths, attain the whole nature, and then experience the culmination of life."

Whether one is Buddhist or Taoist, there is one question regarding meditation that should be asked: "Is there any method that neglects or abandons the physical body, the sensations, emotions, mental states or thoughts associated with it?"

Visualization and Refinement of Thinking

From the Ch'in and Han dynasties to the Wei and Chin dynasties visualization and imaging constitute the main method of Taoism. Ancient Taoist sutras such as *Huang T'ing Nei Wai Chin Ching*, use visualization and imagings as their central principle. Chang Tao Ling in the Han dynasty, the creator of Tien Shu Tao, Kou Ch'ien Chu (another important figure of Tien Shu Tao) in the North Wei dynasty, and the famous Taoist Tau Hong Ching in the South dynasties, use visualization and imagings as their principal methods. Others, such as esoteric Buddhists, employ visualization as a principle of their teaching. Further, conceptualizations and imagings regarding the existence and nature of gods or God are used in the prayers and rituals of many religions.

Transcendental thinking is also mentioned in ancient Taoism. Transcendental thinking and visualization are quite different. Visualization is a method of cultivating the spirit or attitude. Transcendental thinking is a method of cultivating wisdom. Zen Buddhism was established in the South dynasties and continued until the Sui and Tang dynasties. During the Sung and Yuan dynasties the *Hua Tou* and other methods were developed. *Hua Tou* is a Zen Buddhist practice method. The first way of *Hua Tou* is to repeat a sentence continuously and to watch it with the mind. For example, one might inquire, "Who am I...? Who am I...?" Observe the pauses...; eventually one can stop the mad coursing of the mind and extend the periods of silence to infinity. The second way to work with *Hua Tou*, or "word head," is to repeat an inquiry with a strong questioning mood without seeking the answer by means of ratiocinative thinking. These methods are alternate ways of transcendental thinking.

Visualization and transcendental thinking methods involve neither the transmutation of *ch'i* method that prevailed in the Chin, South, and North dynasties, nor the concentration on the cavity (such as concentration on *Tan Tien*) cultivation method that prevailed during the Ming and Ch'ing dynasties. They do not involve the Taoist cultivation method of the transmutation of *ching* into *ch'i*, transmutation of *ch'i* into *shen*, and transmutation of *shen* into Void. Each of these Taoist methods has its own pattern and function. It is unfortunate that those who learn Taoism have confused the different traditions. Some students thought that all they had to do was find a good master who would teach them a hidden secret, and they could become an immortal instantly. They therefore ignored the study of the principles of the Taoist methods. Taoist methods were not organized into a science of immortality with principles, rules, systematic sequences, and methods. As a consequence, these practices lend to calamity rather than to the achievement of immortality.

Although the visualization method is very old, Western mystics employ similar techniques. Western mysticism is supposed to have originated in the legendary Atlantian and Egyptian cultures. In the Orient, in China, the visualization method is supposed to have been handed down from immortals since ancient times. Both of these methods may have originated from the same source. The visualization method seems to be too advanced for easy acceptance by students who are zealous for quick achievements. Visualization (*e.g.*, of God, spirit, heaven) has the dense primitive spirit of religion and, like the teachings of Western mystics, is rich in profound teachings.

7

Concentration on the Ch'iao Cavity in Taoist Meditation

The easiest and most popular methods for training the mind is through concentration on the *Ch'iao* cavity. Strictly speaking, this method emphasizes physiology. Those who use this method assume they should begin with it and use it as the prime technique. In other words, they believe that the body is the basis of Tao, and assume that as long as they can maintain this wonderful knack of *Ch'iao* and successfully concentrate upon and open this *Ch'iao* cavity, they can achieve Tao.

Ch'iao is a location in the body to be concentrated upon but that which does the concentrating is the mind. This method is therefore essentially based on functions of mind.

Several important questions may be asked in this context. Where is the genuine *Ch'iao*? Who should concentrate on *Ch'iao* and who should not? Which *Ch'iao* should those who should concentrate on *Ch'iao* use? Which *Ch'iao* should not be used as a cavity for concentration? These considerations tend to be ignored.

The popular statement, "Open one *Ch'iao* and one hundred *Ch'iao* will open" leads one to believe that it is possible to attain Tao by opening a single *Ch'iao*. But let us consider this. There are nine *Ch'iao* in the human body: two eyes, two ears, two nasal cavities, the mouth, the anus, and the urethra. The seven *Ch'iao* on the head are open. If the seven *Ch'iao* on the head are open, then it seems that the urethra and the anus should open, too. Many people suffer from either serious urinary problems or constipation. From this we can conclude that the *Ch'iao* of meditation are not, as most people have been inclined to believe, the nine *Ch'iao* of the human body.

The meditation method of concentrating on *Ch'iao* sometimes involves concentrating on one of the *acupuncture* points in the body. It is known when a particular acupuncture point is closed, energy still flows freely through the other points. When some points are closed, the main point is still open. Thus, the statement, "Open one *Ch'iao* and one hundred *Ch'iao* will open," is still invalid. Some may claim that it is a *Ch'iao* of Tao which is being referred to here. The *Ch'iao* of Tao is supposed to have no position, no shape, and no actual manifestation, which means it cannot be a location within the body to be meditated upon. Instead, it is a product of the imagination. When one meditates upon the *Ch'iao* of Tao one is using the visualization system of meditation.

In Taoism, the upper, middle and lower *Tan Tien* are generally regarded as the three major *Ch'iao*. The name, *Tan Tien*, did not actually become popular until the Sung and Ming dynasties.

Guard Effects of Concentration

Those who meditate generally prefer to concentrate on the lower *Tan Tien*, and phrases such as "sink the *ch'i* to *Tan Tien*"; "guard the *Tan Tien* with the conscious mind"; "hide the *shen* in *Tan Tien*," are very well known. Some believe that as long as they concentrate on the lower *Tan Tien* they can "withdraw from the *ching* and hold the *ch'i*" or "transmute the *ching* into *ch'i*." Actually, from the standpoint of acupuncture, the *Ch'i Hai* point is actually at the front and the *Ming Men* point at the back of the lower *Tan Tien* and is considered to be the most important part of the adrenal glands.

A big problem is posed by this method. Should a man or woman, whether old or young, healthy or sick, with well-developed or deteriorating and weak adrenal glands concentrate on the lower *Tan Tien*? If a person is not instructed by an experienced and wise master, this technique could cause considerable suffering. Those, for example, who have kidney problems, wet dreams, indulge in excessive masturbation, or suffer from impotence, etc., will aggravate their problems by concentrating on the lower *Tan Tien*. There are, of course, a few exceptions, but they are due to a coincidence and depend on other physiological factors. It is not recommended that a woman meditate on the lower *Tan Tien*, since it might cause menorrhagia or abnormal sexual and mental problems.

One should take into account age, physiology, illnesses, etc., before concentrating on the upper *Ch'iao* such as the point between eyebrows or a point above the head. If one concentrates on the upper *Ch'iao* too much, it might cause high blood pressure, nervous disorders, etc. Some people, because they meditate on the upper *Ch'iao* too often, experience the effect of a reddened face. Such a person regards himself, and others then regard him, as a man of Tao. A man of advanced age should actually be careful of possible cerebrovascular accidents such as the effusion of blood on the brain or apoplexy. If one has a dormant sexual disease and is not thoroughly cured, and if he meditates on the upper *Ch'iao* too long, he could transmit the germs to the brain.

Meditation methods are closely related to psychological and physiological self-healing therapies. When one is seeking longevity, spiritual and mystical cosmic forces are also pertinent. If these highest principles are misunderstood or if these cultivation methods are misapplied, the final result could be tragic. Why not, then, give up meditation and enjoy a natural life?

Principle of Concentration

Concentration of *Ch'iao* does not always produce ill effects, however, and meditation of the *Tan Tien* should not be entirely discarded. Although some people may have apprehensions about practicing this technique, *Tan Tien* does have its special function and it is sometimes desirable for one to concentrate upon it. Meditating on *Ch'iao* is one means of concentrating the thought on a particular point through visualization and this should be clearly understood by anyone who uses this technique.

The function of visualization is to concentrate the will and the mind. It was mentioned previously that *Ch'iao* is the location to be meditated upon; and that which meditates on this location is the mind. This indicates that by the concentration of the mind, one attains the state of unification of spirit. Points on the body can be used for mental concentration for two reasons: First, everyone loves his own body and wishes to improve it; it is a strong representation of ego. So, people are encouraged to work hard when they begin meditation. By working on their bodies they have a chance to attain longevity. Second, psychological and physiological functions are two aspects of a single thing. Mind affects body, and the body also affects the mind. Taoism, therefore, makes use of this body-mind relationship at the outset. The point of concentration on *Ch'iao* develops concentration itself. An individual should attempt to concentrate his entire mind. If he can really concentrate, then the purpose of concentration can be achieved. For example, suppose someone has put a large amount of gold, silver and other treasures in front of you and asks you to concentrate upon guarding it. You may forget to sleep or eat, and may even forget yourself—mind and body—to concentrate solely upon watching these priceless treasures.

Can those who learn quietude and the cultivation of Tao really do well by concentrating on the *Ch'iao*? No, very few can do it well. Most people generally cannot concentrate entirely upon this point. Nervous reactions could cause feelings and sensations at particular points, but chaotic thoughts and illusions may continue to flow, thus preventing the centering of the mind.

Why does this phenomenon occur? Because the mind is strange: the more one attempts to concentrate it, the more scattered it becomes. This can be illustrated with an example from physics. When centripetal force is concentrated to its maximum point, the centrifugal force will naturally react. On the other hand, when centrifugal force reaches its maximum point, the centripetal force will be produced naturally. Analogously, if you grasp your fist very tightly, the reaction of the nerves will cause the fingers to loosen naturally.

Taoism, therefore, compares mental activity to mercury. Mercury tends to be scattered and dispersed. Likewise, it is not easy to achieve unification of spirit by concentrating one's attention on the *Ch'iao*.

If the mind cannot be concentrated, the *ch'i* route absolutely cannot be opened. Some believe that they have opened the *ch'i* route, when this is actually an illusion or a certain physiological feeling. A person can rarely achieve his goals by merely focusing upon physiological feelings.

Concentration on Ch'iao and Refinement of the Ch'i

Concentrating on the *Ch'iao* and refining the *ch'i* are not the same Taoist techniques. Concentrating on *Ch'iao* involves the conscious mind, while refining the *ch'i* consists primarily in refining the breath through the use of the will. No matter what differences there are between these two methods, they all employ the mind. No matter what method is used for meditation, people regard *ch'i* and quietude, *ch'i* and Tao, and *ch'i* and the technique of longevity as having an absolute connection. Those who specialize in yoga and *ch'i kung* emphasize *ch'i*. Tai Chi Chuan, which became popular at the end of the Ch'ing dynasty, involves the principle of sinking the *ch'i* into *Tan Tien*. Many meditate in an attempt to guide their breath toward the *Tan Tien,* hoping that the *ch'i* will sink into the *Tan Tien* so that they can thereby enter the Tao.

There are many methods of *ch'i kung* and many techniques of Taoism. Those familiar with these methods ask how they can condense the *ch'i* into *Tan Tien* or other locations. If one squeezes air into a ball, can he expect the air to remain in a particular portion in the ball? This is impossible. The body is like a ball. The *ch'i* circulates everywhere. Only a seriously ill person who has obstacles to some function might unwittingly have *ch'i* locked in a given location. The *ch'i* of a healthy person would never be in this condition.

Some people believe that those who work at concentrating on *Ch'iao* or refining *ch'i* can voluntarily keep the *ch'i* in a certain position. This, however, is merely an illusion. The sensation of retaining *ch'i* in a particular location is actually just the glutting of nerves and blood vessels, which occurs as a consequence of intense mental concentration on a certain point of the body. *Ch'i* cannot be coagulated in a particular location. This suggests that understanding the nature of genuine *ch'i* is one of the most difficult problems accompanying the practice of meditation.

Part II
The Nature and Reactions of **Ch'i**

8

The Nature of Ch'i

What is *ch'i?* This is really a problem. Three characters are used in Taoism to try to explain the meaning of *ch'i.* The ancient character for *ch'i* is 炁. The upper portion of this character, 旡, means no-thing. The lower part of this character, ㆍㆍㆍ, means fire. Ancient Taoist sutras employ this character which means *no fire* to indicate *ch'i.* (See also p. 9.)

Taoism and ancient Chinese culture are closely associated. The five elements, the celestial stems, and the earthly branches especially are widely used in Taoism. Among the five elements, heart or mind belong to fire. To say that *ch'i* is no fire (no desire or lust) means that when one attains mental quietude and has no thoughts or worries, then real *ch'i* is generated.

The second character for *ch'i* is 气. It is written in the ancient style and represents air in nature.

The third character for *ch'i* is 氣. This more modern character represents air, breath and gas.

Before the Tang dynasty, there were some special Taoist techniques that enabled one to swallow the *ch'i.* By concentrating the mind and breathing in a certain way, one might attain a state "enabling him to communicate with the spirit of heaven and earth."[5] These techniques evolved into the many *ch'i kung* methods of a later age. The aim of practicing *ch'i kung* methods is to arouse the latent energy of genuine *ch'i*. But if one attends solely to the breathing exercises, he will never attain the highest achievements of *ch'i kung* and body yoga.

What is genuine *ch'i*? It is difficult to describe. In yoga it is called spirit energy (shakti); the serpent power (kundalini). In Tibetan esoteric teachings it is called spirit force or spirit heat. In modern terminology we can call it the prime energy of life or energy. Here energy does not mean the physical energy which many people believe to be electrical energy or electricity. This is a misunderstanding, since the ultimate nature of energy is not the function of a material thing. But, discussing this further would involve us in the central disputes of philosophy and science which cannot be resolved here.

Given this, it may sound as though there is no relationship between mental quietude and *ch'i*. This is not the case. In the Chinese culture, *quiet sitting* is a general term. The growth and development of a human body can be compared to the growth and development of a pine tree. The trunk, branches, clusters of needle shaped leaves, and the cones develop from a germinated seed and unfold in an orderly sequence. Although a pine can be dwarfed (by growing it in a small shallow pot), or cultivated into ornamental shapes (as in the case of a bonsai), the growth and development of all pines is basically the same. Similarily, those who work hard and practice regularly will notice that meditation leads to physiological manifestations of *ch'i*. The phenomena of *ch'i* varies for different persons but it usually results in the production of mental images. Although different people will have different sorts of mental images, nearly everyone will have to deal with the appearances of images and illusions.

If one is more or less familiar with terms such as the eight extra meridians, large circulation, small circulation (*i.e.,* the circulation of *ch'i* along *Jen* and *Tu Mai*), K'an (☵) and Li (☲), lead and mercury, dragon and tiger, yin and yang, etc., these

---

[5]This method for the cultivation of *ch'i* leads to the same achievements as the practice of ancient yoga.

vague concepts will condition the nature and quality of one's illusions. When the reactions of *ch'i* begin, they are naturally influenced by a person's preconceptions which lead him to experience unfamiliar feelings which will conform to his particular state of mind.

Ch'i Relates to Air

Most people who learn meditation tend to associate breathing with *ch'i*. They therefore assume that air is the center of internal *ch'i* in the human body. From the viewpoint of meditation the effect of breathing is limited to the upper part of the diaphragm. The reaction of *ch'i* inside the body is not merely connected with breath.

The function of breathing is well known. For those who cultivate *ch'i*, air is like the material used to kindle a fire. The latent infinite energy of the body is like a primitive treasure: it comes with life. But unless it is refined in a reasonable way, this latent life-energy will never be kindled and will dissipate at death.

The *dhyana* teachings of Hinayana Buddhism classify the breathing of air and the latent energy of the human body into three ordered categories.

1) *Wind* This indicates the ordinary function of the respiratory system and air. In other words, people depend on breath to maintain life. This is the state of air known as "wind."

2) *Ch'i* This indicates that after refinement through meditation, the breath per se becomes light, easy and slow.

3) *Hsi* Through the highly advanced refinement of meditation the breath becomes so slight that it almost stops. At this stage the inward and outward movement of the respiratory system ceases to function. Breathing through other parts of the body, however, is not completely stopped. A natural breath starts to function from the lower abdomen to the lower *Tan Tien*. This is *Hsi*. Later, the Taoists call it *Tai Hsi* (the breathing of an embryo in the womb). Some schools of thought even believe that mind and *Hsi* are interdependent.

These principles and practices were developed from the *dhyana* cultivation method of Hinayana Buddhism during the Sui and Tang dynasties. They were absorbed by the Tien Tai sect, included in the *Chih* and *Kuan* cultivation methods, and with modifications and changes added, retained popularity. Although the practice methods of Taoism before the Sui and Tang dynasties also emphasized cultivation of *ch'i,* there were no theories about the interconnections of *Tai Hsi,* mind and *Hsi* at that time. Some pseudo-Taoist sutras purported to be sutras of the Wei and Chin dynasties, occasionally mention these theories. These sutras, however, are deceptive and should not be trusted.

9

Reactions of Ch'i During Meditation

We shall now discuss the relationship between meditation and *ch'i* and their functions. First, one should realize that what is described below pertains to sexually mature adults, to those who already have a sex life. It cannot apply to immature children, to young girls who have not yet begun their monthly cycle, or to young boys who have not yet experienced the flow of semen.

The physical reactions that take place during meditation are classified below into a first, second, third reaction and so on. This does not necessarily mean that the reactions will take place according to this sequence. Some will follow this sequence; some will not. It depends on one's mental and physical conditions.

Numbness or Swelling in Legs

The first reaction a person feels at the beginning of meditation practice is that he cannot calm his mind, and he experiences strange sensations from purely physiological reactions. The mental aspects of meditation are not covered in this book since the discussion is limited to physiological reactions.

According to statistics, eighty to ninety percent of beginners first experience a numbness or swelling of the legs. This will cause one to feel aches or soreness, and even disquiets the mind. From the standpoint of common sense, most people assume this is caused by the compression of the blood vessels in the legs and therefore it is undesirable.

From the standpoint of empirical observation and the principles of meditation, these phenomena are not, however, caused completely by the pressure on blood vessels. In reality they result from the response and movement of the *ch'i*. Because the *ch'i* cannot flow freely between the blood vessels, muscles and tendons, one sometimes experiences numbness, aches and swelling in the legs. These sensations indicate that there are obstacles in the *ch'i* routes of *Yin Ch'iao* and *Yang Ch'iao*. When one can no longer endure this feeling, he can loosen the legs. After awhile he will experience fresh, unfamiliar, comfortable feelings. When one has advanced to a certain stage in meditation, no matter whether he crosses his legs or not, he will always experience these fresh and wonderful euphoric feelings. At this stage, a person will be able to cross his legs to meditate for long periods without feeling any obstructions. This comfortable feeling of euphoria or ecstacy gradually becomes stronger and stronger.

Strengthening of Genital Functions

Here we should distinguish between 1) renal or kidney functions, and 2) genital functions. For an adult, the second reaction to meditation will generally start from the renal parts (including the loins and waist) and, after a time of practice, the genital or reproductive organs will also respond. A young man's reaction begins in the genital organ.

The reaction of the renal organ is such that during or after meditation a man will experience a swollen filling sensation, ache, numbness, etc., at his waist and back. Those who are impotent, or who experience premature ejaculation (ejaculatis praecox) or nocturnal emissions (perhaps due to kidney problems), may aggravate the difficulties through meditation. Some might even lose semen while defecating, micturating, or meditating. The occurrence of such phenomena accompany kidney deterioration or adrenal, genital and pituitary gland problems, as well as neurasthenia. Women who have kidney problems may experience the phenomenon of leukorrhea.

Meditation does not *cause* these undesirable effects. They are due to old illnesses. The nerves and *ch'i* routes around the renal and waist areas constitute obstacles to the *ch'i* that is generated during meditation, which must work to open and pass these areas. If one understands this principle and has instruction from a good master about suitable remedies, these problems can all be overcome, and one will eventually recover health in the renal organs. If instruction from a good master is not available, then one should stop meditation until health is recovered, and then begin meditation again. If these phenomena recur, once again stop meditation. By repeating this procedure, although meditation is necessarily intermittent, one may eventually recover his health.

Remedies cannot be described here because they depend upon the individual and the specific problems. Remedies involve medical theory and physical exercises which are too complicated to describe. The most important point is that one should refrain from sexual activities in order to clear up these problems. If one could abolish sexual desires, that would in itself be an excellent remedy. One can often recover health faster in this case. Depending on gender, age and physical strength, the reactions that take place during recovery vary and are often complicated.

The reactions of the genital or reproductive organs are such that during, or after, meditation, the penis is suddenly tumescent for a long time; at the same time a jumping sensation may be experienced in the small capillary nerves around the testicles, and a vibration may be felt in the prostate gland and perineum area. For women, fibrillation or contraction of the uterus and swelling of the breasts sometimes occur. According to some Taoist schools, this indicates the return of yang. Thus, one could apply his or her mind to sóme breathing exercises to guide circulation of the yang.

If one does not connect the physical phenomena of meditation to sexual fantasies or lustful cravings, then the sexual manifestations could indicate a very good condition. This shows that one's pituitary, adrenal, and genital glands have become more vital and complement the health.

Regardless of gender or age, almost everyone has sexual impulses triggered by this phenomenon. These sexual impulses may then create feelings of lethargy or tumescence in the head, or an annoying feeling in the chest, etc. If one has sexual intercourse when this occurs, he or she will not only waste all the benefits of previous meditation, but may also cause damage as a consequence of increased vitality. If one has no sexual fantasy or sexual activity, then what Lao Tze said about a baby is generally applicable, "To not know the intercourse of male and female and yet have an erection, this is the arising of *ching.*" This triggers the latent life force and initiates the development of *ch'i*. In general, almost everyone advances to this step and then encounters great difficulty passing beyond it. If one does not know the method for remedying this, even if he can repress himself for a long time, it will eventually develop into illness or dis-ease.[6]

About thirty years ago, a middle-aged male friend said that he meditated with his wife at night. Whenever the phenomenon of sexual arousal occurred as a consequence of meditating, he felt his wife was much more attractive than under ordinary circumstances. He therefore chose to enjoy sexual intercourse rather than to seek the rewards of sexual continence. Another man, in his sixties, while meditating in the mountains, tried to

[6]The damage is similar to that caused by avoiding ejaculation during intercourse. Being able to meditate for a long time without any reactions in the genital organs indicates that such an individual's life force is close to being abated. After a while a person's mind becomes a stagnant pool and his body becomes withered.

allay his sexual feelings in many ways including immersion in cold water. The means he selected proved ineffective, so he abandoned his meditation in favor of the relief which relations with his wife could afford. These two cases clearly illustrate how meditation increases one's sexual desires and they led me to search for some sort of solution to this common problem.

The remedy for the reaction of the genital organs during meditation is very complicated. For those who are willing to focus their time and energies on meditation, the most simple and effective method of alleviating these problems is to decrease the amount of food one eats. Even a fast for a short period can be helpful. One of the precepts of Buddhism is not to eat after noon. This precept is not derived merely from a static regulation. A Chinese proverb says, "'One starts to think about sex when one is warm and full of food; one tends to think of stealing when one is cold and hungry." However, fasting or eating less is not easy.

Editor's Note: Since Western readers might otherwise be disconcerted by the possible implications of the author's remarks on sexuality, it seems appropriate to clarify his views.

The author is not against sexual activities and does not believe sexual practices are incompatible with the cultivation of Tao. Tantra, for example, is a cultivation method that involves (and is primarily based upon) sexual union. The main point here is that one's vitality is greatly increased by meditation practice. Further, since one's vital energy is closely connected with one's sexual energy (if they are not in fact the same), increased vitality will increase one's sexual desire and urges. Thus, sexual urges arising from meditation practice exceed one's "normal" range. When a person reaches this point in meditation practice he has two choices: he can release the accumulated energy by engaging in sexual activities (and since his urges and desires will be unusually strong, he will have a tendency to overindulge, dispersing the energy it has taken him so long to accumulate); or he can utilize this energy to advance to another level in meditation. The decision is entirely up to the student, but since Professor Nan is primarily interested in meditation he would, if asked, probably recommend that the student use this energy to advance in meditation.

Western students are familiar with the idea that sexual energy can be transformed into spiritual energy—nuns, monks, bishops, cardinals, and many religious leaders are dedicated to the practice of celibacy for this very reason. And Western students are also familiar with the Freudian view that sublimated sexual energy can be transformed into creative energy and utilized for advancing one's work.

We are aware of spiritual and creative advances that appear to have been made as a consequence of sublimating sexual energies. Similarly, the author suggests that sexual energy is a form of vital energy that can be used to advance to a higher level if one refrains from sexual activities during certain stages of meditation.

Reactions on Back and Scapula

In the course of meditation practice, or at any other time, one may experience heaviness or aching in the back or scapular regions, or sense tautness of the nerves around these areas. This is the third reaction to meditation and there are two main causes: The *ch'i* is ascending through *Tu Mai*—the governing vessel—the central nerve system in the spinal cord, or it is a reaction of an illness.

1) The reactions of illness: This applies to those who are weak and have illnesses or to those of advanced years. These illnesses include lung disease, gastric and hepatic disorders, cardiac disease and various other latent conditions. If a person has these diseases, at a certain stage of meditation he will feel aching and heaviness like a strong pressure on the back, flaccidity and lack of strength or aching around the waist. Cramps or convulsive contractions may occur in the back, or congestion may occur in the shoulder, or aching may occur causing one to perspire, feel chills and fever.

If these phenomena occur, one should understand that this trouble is not produced by meditation. The quiet in meditation is, after all, a means of rest. No one is apt to get sick from merely taking rest. One should be glad, however, because without the test of meditation, one might not have realized that one already had some sort of disease. The pains one feels show the self-healing effect of increased vitality and indicate that the disease is still curable and has not progressed to the extent that there is no remedying it. For example, a man may not initially feel any pain from a very serious wound and yet when the wound begins to heal, he will. Similarly, when a man first catches a common cold, the germs of the cold are still latent; there are no symptoms. When the symptoms of the cold are evident, the cold is already going away.

If these phenomena appear in the course of meditation practice, one should take medical treatments in addition to the healing involved in meditation. So long as one has the will to persist through these crises, the crises can lead to a healthier condition.

2) The reactions of *ch'i*: If one is normal and healthy, after the first and second reactions mentioned above, one will

naturally enter the stage of feeling a swelling sensation around the back and scapular areas. Or, one may have the feeling that there is a strong force moving with difficulty along the spinal cord which is prevented from pushing upward. One may also hope that these forces will push through the obstruction so that one can finally feel relaxed and comfortable. In Taoism, this phenomenon is called the River Chariot which rolls to the location of the *Chia Chih*. This occurs during the process of opening the *Tu Mai*. This is the stage where the *ch'i* starts to reach the Huang Yang point.

If one cannot release his mind and attain the state of forgetting the body, the pressure will become stronger and stronger. Whenever this phenomenon occurs, a person's attention will automatically focus on the back and one may attempt to use the force of consciousness or imagination to push the pressure upward. Because of the concentration of attention here, the brain and stomach nerves will become tighter and tighter. The heart will contract and the uncomfortable feeling in the back will be increased.

Some schools of Taoism teach one to guide the *ch'i* with consciousness, to push it through or to drive it. Students are to imagine the progression of the River Chariot and engage in taking deep, long, but tiny breaths (6 × 6, thirty-six deep breaths; or 9 × 9, eighty-one deep breaths) which numerically match the Big and Small circulations of heaven. Or they are to use some Taoism or yoga exercises to guide the passage of *ch'i* through this location.

Although these direction exercises have a temporary effect and make one feel that something passes through the *Chia Chih* to rush up to *Yu Chen* (*i.e.,* the back of head), it is only the mental force that changes this physical feeling, but *it is definitely not the phenomenon of ch'i passing through the Chia Chih.*

If one can attain the state of "forgetting his own body," or apply his wisdom in an attempt to forget his feelings and remain quiet without taking any mental action, then there will be a moment when suddenly, like a switch making a contact, all the tension is gone and the mind and body are loose and at ease. From this turning point one will experience the state of breadth and brightness of mind and fullness of spirit. A person whose back is humped at this stage will naturally straighten his waist and back, stretch his chest, and his breath will become smoother. For those who are born with advanced scoliosis or who have it as a result of an external wound, this is a difficult situation.[7]

At this stage a person will be so charged that he will not fall asleep easily. Since he may be used to sleeping at a fixed time, he might assume that he has insomnia and feel frightened. It should be understood that this is not the insomnia of ordinary people. One should let nature take its course. If one cannot fall asleep, just don't go to bed.

Reactions in Head

The fourth reaction occurs in the head and these are more complicated than those which occur in other parts of the body. According to traditional Chinese medicine, "the head is the chief of the yangs." Its functions are therefore very great. From the viewpoint of Taoism, the head includes the *Yu Chen* at the back of the head and the *Ni Huang Palace* at the top of the head, both of which are very important. From the standpoint of modern medical science, the head is related to the nerves of the cerebellum, cerebrum, and the diencephalon and pituitary gland organs. These relationships are very complicated. The head is also directly associated with the nerve cells of the (five) senses. Several serious difficulties may therefore arise when one reaches this stage. One could, for example, begin to hallucinate.

For the purpose of discussion, the head regions will be considered in the following sequence: 1) the back of the head, 2) the front of the head, and 3) the center of the head.

The reactions at the back of the head: Some people indulge in a quiet state of mind; they regard the solitary quietness of mind as the only effect of meditation. For these people advanced

---

[7]It is impossible to give any advice regarding these conditions, since the treatment would require a discussion of material far beyond the scope of this book.

discussion is not feasible. *Physical reactions are a necessary concomitant of meditation.* After the stages where the *ch'i* passes the genital organs, the waist and the back, the *ch'i* will naturally ascend to the back of the head. The most common reaction when the *ch'i* reaches this point is that one will not feel completely clear and bright mentally, but experience a kind of lethargy even to the point of dozing but not sleeping. For Buddhists who practice *dhyana* or *Chih* and *Kuan,* this phenomenon is considered one of the obstacles to the cultivation of Tao, because in *Chih* and *Kuan* it is believed that one should keep one's mind bright and clear all the time.

Some schools of Taoism misunderstand this phenomenon and take it to be the state of *Hung Tung*—that is, the brewing of the life force in its primitive state. Or they take it to be *Tso Wang*—that is, sitting in a mental state of abstraction, forgetting oneself and everything else. This state is not, however, really *Hung Tung* or *Tso Wang,* although it is similar to them.

Because Taoists emphasize the cultivation of the body, they take the physiological life energy to be the starting point, and therefore believe this state of lethargy is a wonderful phenomenon.

The Buddhist begins cultivation by working on his mind, intends to drop the *satkayadrsti,* i.e., the illusion that his body or self is real, and hopes to enter Original Nature directly. Consequently Buddhists regard dozing, as well as rampant thinking, as a hindrance to the bright and clear phenomena of their Original Nature. They assume these conditions are obstacles to their goal. As long as one understands the principles, it is not important to decide if they are right or wrong.

The basic differences between Buddhism and Taoism have to do with their starting methods and initial aims, which are not the same. One cannot avoid the effects of the relationship between the mind and body. Even if one does not emphasize body when entering into a state of quietude, bodily activities cannot be ignored. One must depend upon the body if one hopes to break the shell of its bondage. Therefore the theory of "using the false body to cultivate the real" was promoted by Taoists during the Sung and Yuan dynasties.

When *ch'i* ascends to the back of the head, one feels lethargic. A person might fall asleep if he does not have sufficient bodily strength, or if he is physically and mentally tired, and he might not be able to retain the meditation posture. This may occur because of insufficient oxygen in the brain. Yawning naturally accompanies the state of being tired and dozing. If one has enough bodily strength and the *ch'i* ascends to the back of the head, one may notice darkness in front of the eyes when half asleep. Gradually a dreamlike state occurs, and images eventually appear. This happens because *ch'i* affects the nerves at the back of the head, which then affect the optic nerves. Many people have dream images accompanied by feelings of love and joy or sadness and dread. These images and feelings match subconscious functions which give rise to one's mental states, thoughts and concepts. States of *Mara,* or demonic delusion, may occur at this stage. These states depend upon one's wisdom, thought, personality, psychological propensities, and physiological condition. They are very complicated. Without the guidance of a very perceptive master, and in the absence of self-confidence, healthy intelligence, and correct thinking, a person may be led down the wrong road.

When a person understands this, he can ignore phenomena of this sort, knowing that light follows the darkness. After passing through this stage one feels somewhat more awake. Points of light, like a fluorescent star, may appear in front of your eyes, sparkling in different shapes and colors. These colors and lights are connected with your physiology and will be discussed later in more detail.

If one is not internally healthy, has a latent brain illness, disorders in any one of the five sense organs, indigestion, inflammation of the intestinal tract, intestinal and stomach disorders or some other disease, then this meditative state could cause redness of the cornea or a ringing or feeling of pressure in the ears. Those with bad teeth may feel pain or shaking in the teeth. Latent colds and other problems could erupt, such as inflammation of the lymph nodes or pain in some region of the brain. But, everyone should realize that latent diseases may be discovered, but are not actually caused by meditation. *In other words, meditation increases inner vitality and begins to heal the body. By* persistent meditation and appropriate medical treatment, one can recover one's health. Therefore, since ancient times it has been believed that a person who cultivates the Tao should also understand medical science.

Reactions in Back of the Head

By the time *ch'i* reaches the back of the head, one will have made great advances in meditation and should feel joyful. This is the fifth reaction; it is a complicated stage and is often accompanied by a great deal of trouble. Everyone should exercise caution and good judgment during this stage. It may also help to study some auxiliary methods of meditation and cultivation, such as the *ch'i* route, acupuncture, and medicinal drugs. This stage is joyous, however, because after passing it one can open the *ch'i* route of the central nervous system and cerebrum. But, those who have a deteriorated physical constitution, brain disease, or mental illness tend to go in the wrong direction at this stage. A middle-aged or elderly person might have uncomfortable feelings similar to hypertension. However, there is absolutely no possibility that this stage is the actual cause of hypertension. If a person attempts to concentrate on the upper *Tan Tien,* then his face will become red, a symptom of hypertension. Most people tend to assume that a reddened face is the effect of the cultivation of Tao, but one should not believe it.

When *ch'i* reaches the back of the head, a person might hear wonderful inner sounds or experience ringing or pressure in his ears. This phenomenon is produced by *ch'i* working to open the *ch'i* route in the brain. The vibration or trembling of *ch'i* causes some brain wave activity. If one's intelligence is not clear and bright enough, then illusions deep inside the subconscious will result.

One who has deep religious beliefs may have illusions of hearing the voice of God or Buddha. Often the voice will speak of the past or future, and this *a priori* information may be quite

correct, at least in small things. Thus, one might believe he has
clairaudience. Whatever is heard is actually just a big assembly;
it is a mixing of previous experience—what has been seen,
heard, thought and known before. This kind of clairaudience
could be used to predict small matters, but it will not work on
big events at all. If one clings to the idea that these voices are
real, he will fall into a state of *Mara,* or illusion. This shows that
the mind is receptive to impressions but this is not a genuine
instance of clairaudience. A person should not be puzzled or
moved by this reaction. Instead, he should sometimes swallow
the saliva and release the feelings in his head. This requires a
strong mind and a persistent will. By guiding the *ch'i* downward
one will pass this stage and enter the next.

Ideally, one should use the Taoist's internal *Kung Fu,* employ
the special body exercises and adjustments of yoga and esoteric
Buddhism and have required medical treatments when necessary.

Whenever transformations of *ch'i* occur during various
stages of meditation, a person's attention will often be focused
on his feelings. When the *ch'i* reaches the brain, attention to
these feelings becomes especially strong. This may cause a
contraction of the lower abdomen, an upward contraction of the
diaphragm, or a loss of appetite and temporary constipation. It is
all right to use an anti-inflammatory agent or cathartic
occasionally. It is better, however, to have some knowledge and
experience of medical science regardless of whether it is
Chinese or Western folk medicine.

According to Chinese medicine, the lungs and the large
intestine are closely related to each other. The heart, small
intestine, and bladder are also believed to be closely related
to each other. Sometimes one can use breathing exercises to
smooth the *ch'i* in the lungs to help cure constipation. Too much
tension in the heart may change the bladder; sometimes
abnormal urination, such as incontinence in the case of extreme
fright, will occur. This verifies the fact that mental states can
affect physiology. Thus, if a person cannot find a wise master
for instruction, he should refer to medical sources in an attempt
to help himself.

Reactions in the Front of the Head

After the *ch'i* passes the back of the head, it reaches the front of the head. The sixth reaction to meditation is not as complicated as the fifth which we just discussed. The most typical phenomenon is a feeling of swelling in both temples and, again, a desire to doze. Those whose strength and *ch'i* are relatively abundant, often experience a swelling sensation or slight stimulation at the top of the nose, and at the central point between the eyebrows. However, thoughts and images will naturally be decreased and weakened. Although one may feel slightly lethargic, physiological and mental pressures are considerably less than those symptoms described in previous paragraphs. However, discomfort could be caused by possible congestion in the eyes and red threads in the conjunctiva.

Whether a person opens or closes his eyes, he will see lights like the sun or moon or even fluorescence. The light will be either stationary or flashing. Sometimes one can observe people and events occurring inside this light and one will realize what will happen in the future. Some people think this is clairvoyance. Some, through misunderstanding the teachings of Buddhism, believe that this phenomena of light is the light of their Original Nature. Zen Buddhists denounce this as the delusion of light, and Taoists also regard this as illusion. This light is actually due to the fluctuations of *ch'i* in the brain that induces thoughts or images and alters brain wave patterns. This phenomenon is only temporary and should not be considered real.

Seeing uncertain and changing colors, either in visions or dreams, may be due to latent diseases in the viscera. If the kidneys and related genital nerves deteriorate or are weakened and diseased, this will be reflected by the phenomena of light seen in the form of black points or solid black. If the liver is diseased, the color will appear to be blue; if the heart is diseased, the color seen will be red; if the lungs are not healthy, the color one sees will be white; if the spleen or stomach are diseased, the color seen will be yellow; if the gallbladder is diseased the color seen will be green.

From the standpoint of Chinese mystics, seeing black in dreams, visions or hallucinations usually indicates trouble and disaster. The color blue indicates sadness, grief or sorrow, and green indicates hindrance from hallucinations, or *Mara*. Red indicates inauspiciousness. Yellow and white are auspicious, indicating calm persons and smooth situations. However, these are not fixed rules.

One should realize that all phenomena are caused by the mind. Mind can distort matters as well as transform them. If we straighten the body and mind so that they are right, states of *Mara*, or hallucination, can be transformed into *states of a saint*. It is all a matter of mind. The correct principle is to reflect and check upon one's own mental behavior.

If one does not know how to guide and adjust the *ch'i* suitably in the front of the head, then the *ch'i* will rush to the nose and activate latent sinus diseases. Mucous may drip from the sinus cavities continuously. One school of Taoism considers this losing the *ching* and *ch'i*. Therefore, one should voluntarily inhibit the discharge so that nothing vital will be lost. Inhibiting the discharge of mucous from the nose might prove to be effective for some purposes; however, the question is how one can inhibit this loss. First, it is essential to run a medical test on the mucous to make sure that it contains no toxins or bacteria.

Only if it is medically determined that the mucous is harmless can one sniff it back and, with impunity, allow it to drain into the stomach. Under such clinically approved conditions, the nose-running might stop after several days and one may enter a better state of meditation. Some people do not know that such treatments are feasible and will tolerate mucous discharge for many years until it induces another disease.

Many monks and Taoists who advanced to the stage where the *ch'i* reaches the front of the head do not know how to treat this mucous discharge from the nose. They like to cite the cases of Dan Ts'an and Han Shan, who, in order to dispel attachment to etiquette and attendant squeamish feelings, permitted the discharge of their nasal mucous to reach their shoulders. This phenomenon bothered me for three years until one day I suddenly realized the possibility of inhaling and swallowing the mucous as a means of treating the problem. After treating it in this way I was able to advance further. My experience might prove to be valuable to those who are approaching this stage in this meditation. After one passes this stage, one will begin to smell fragrances. These are normal fragrances from one's viscera and not mystical fragrances from the environment.

Reactions in the Top of the Head

At the time when *ch'i* passes beyond the front of the head and rushes to the nose (keep in mind that one can direct it back at will) it will rotate like the shape of ꝙ. In this seventh reaction it comes to the center of the cerebrum and cerebellum before it moves upward to the top of the head. When this occurs one naturally straightens one's posture and experiences a great *samadhi*.

Taoists call the top of the head *Ni Huang Palace* and yogis call it *The Crown*. Some Taoists believe that this is the phenomenon of opening up the *Tu Mai* completely. But, this is not the case. These are merely changes along the *Tu Mai* that accompany the initial opening of the central nervous system. This is followed by stimulating the function of the top of the head to enhance the uniform distribution of endocrine secretions. However, at this step some people will have temporary pain or a heavy sensation at the top of the head, as though it were being pressed by something, or they may feel extreme tightness. This is due to the fact that the *ch'i* route in the head is not completely open, or because one's attention is unduly attracted to feelings and sensations and one is preoccupied with them. If one can divert his attention and forget his head and let it be natural, then a very comfortable and refreshing feeling will gradually be generated and will move downward from the top of the head. This phenomenon is the forerunner of *Ching An*, which means lightness and calmness, in Buddhist meditation, including *Chih* and *Kuan*. At this stage, thoughts and illusions are weakened and therefore one enters the first step of *samadhi*.

If sweet cool saliva descends, it is the endocrine secretion from the pituitary gland. It is described by Taoists as *T'i Hu Kuang Ting*, an inauguration or consecration by sprinkling a rich liquor skimmed from boiled butter on the head. It is also sometimes referred to as a "Sweet dew spray over Mountain Sumeru," or "The nectar of liquid jade." Taoists regard this as a tonic wine for rejuvenation and long life. Although this sounds very mystical or hypothetical, it really has the effect of healing disease and contributing to a long life. It might stimulate one's appetite, and a person may find that he can readily digest and completely absorb the nutrients of food, even after eating too heavily. At the same time, one will feel very little hunger even if he goes without eating, or else he will be able to swallow air to dispel his hunger. Of course, at this stage a person is full of spirit which will be evidenced by his shining countenance.

In addition, when the *ch'i* is really passing through the head there will be sounds like "Pi Pi Pai Pai" in the head. This is the reaction of nerves induced by the *ch'i* working to open up the paths. The sound is nothing strange; it is like the sound one hears when he covers his ears with his palms and hears his own heart and the circulation of blood. However, if one's attention is absorbed by these sounds or if there is some latent disease in Upper Warmer,[8] then one will want to shake his head quite often. If a person does not know the treatment for this, or if he cannot deflect his attention from it, it will become a kind of sick state. On the other hand, if the meditator knows how to be calm and quiet and can ignore this feeling, then he will naturally attain the *Ching An* described above. There are some people who experience this phenomenon in their youth without practicing meditation. One might think of it as a kind of neurosis but if it is not stimulated by other factors, it is not a disease.

If the reactions involving the waist, back, back of the head, top of the head, and the area behind the eyebrows in the center of the head take place, someone might suppose that he has

[8]The Upper Warmer is part of the Triple Heater Meridian known to acupuncturists. The Triple Heater includes the Upper Warmer, located in the thorax, the Middle Warmer, located in the upper abdomen, and the Lower Warmer, located in the lower abdomen.

opened the *Tu Mai*. However, these reactions do not indicate that the *Tu Mai* is opened; they are merely the initial physiological reactions. When the *Tu Mai* is actually opened, special symptoms will occur, and always in constant response to the *Jen Mai*. The previously mentioned physiological feelings and sensations are only minor matters.

When the *ch'i* is circulating in the head, one often has a sensation of swelling, pain or other uncomfortable feelings. Or, a person might sleep very soundly but very frequently or remain asleep for a very long time. The *ch'i* affects the orbital nerves, the tympanic membrane, the conjunctiva and the nasal cavity and it sometimes causes disease-like symptoms. Further some might even feel that the head is heavy and the feet are light, or become quick-tempered, easily angered, constipated or overstimulated so that they cannot fall asleep or cannot sleep restfully. Readers should not be frightened by the possibility of such bad effects following from opening the *Tu Mai* through meditation. Everyone will not experience all the phenomena described; what happens will depend upon a person's sex, age, and individual mental and physiological states. Further, feelings of pain caused by meditation are not actually the pains of a real disease although they are similar to them.

In conclusion, by the time the *ch'i* ascends to the head, one will already have experienced a certain number of effects. One should calm the mind in order to maintain quietude and await the *ch'i*'s descent to the larynx, the epigastric area, the chest area, the stomach area, the lower *Tan Tien* and renal area from which *ch'i* flows to the apex of the genital organs. This sequence is the *Jen Mai* of Taoist and Chinese medical arts, and it corresponds to the major areas of the autonomic nervous system in Western medical science.

10
How to Open Up **Jen Mai**

Whether the *ch'i* descends to pass along the *Jen Mai* according to the sequence mentioned above is a practical problem. Those who practice meditation and the cultivation of Tao usually follow the texts of Taoism as well as other meditation books. Such people are often without any real experience or are preoccupied with their own viewpoint, which is often made up of entirely subjective illusions. Consequently, they regard the utilization of the *Jen Mai* as the step following the engagement of *Tu Mai*. The technique of willfully attempting to guide the *ch'i* by one's own consciousness leads one to expect to have this impression or to draw this conclusion. However, from the viewpoint of the cultivation of Tao through meditation, this is a shallow concept. This chapter will attempt to clarify the way in which *ch'i* passes through the *Jen Mai* so that the reader will be able to understand and integrate this material.

The Center of Jen Mai is "Middle House"

According to Taoism and the Chinese medical arts, "Middle House" is an abstract term. The major area of its operation is the stomach which belongs to earth. This is derived from the abstract concepts of yin yang, and the eight trigrams of the *I Ching,* of the five elements—water, earth, fire, wood, metal.

There were two schools of Chinese medicine during the Chin and Yuan dynasties. One emphasized the treatment of stomach *ch'i.* The other usually emphasized the nourishment of the kidneys, which were associated with the element of water: *K'an.* These primitive concepts are all derived from the abstract symbolism of ying yang and the eight trigrams. The four diagrams and five elements are all based on earth. The nine houses and eight trigrams cannot be disassociated from *Jen* which forms the basis of these theories. *Jen* is one of the celestial stems and belongs to the water element.

The spleen and stomach are very important to one's health, longevity, and cultivation of Tao. The first serious warning for any disease is a change in appetite. For example, people who have a cold or the flu don't have a good appetite, which indicates intestinal and stomach problems. But, catching a cold or the flu does not make much difference to those who have good digestion. The stomach is connected to the esophagus above and connected to the large intestine below and it affects the function of the kidneys and the sexual glands.

The first sign of the opening of *Jen Mai* is that there is *ch'i* bubbling or vibrating in the intestines and stomach; one feels these vibrations like air bubbling inside the stomach. After this initial reaction there are two possibilities. First, a person might have a strong appetite in which case he should not overeat. Instead, he should pay attention to eating wholesome nutritious food which he can easily digest and absorb. Second, one might not have an appetite and feel full of *ch'i*. In this case he should eat less or go on a fast until his appetite returns. Then he should eat less food but eat more frequently.

In addition to the first symptom described above, one might experience hiccoughs, yawning, venting intestinal gases, or all three at the same time. Some people believe that venting the fermenting gases of flatulency is tantamount to a loss of vitality, or *ch'i*, either because they misunderstood the Taoist sutras or have been misinformed by their teachers. Consequently, they usually try vigorously to contract the sphincter muscle to prevent it. This causes the accumulation of gas which irritates the viscera and results in constipation, anal fistula and other diseases of the viscera. Actually the theory that one should not allow his vitality, or *ch'i*, to dissipate is not applicable at this stage. Thus, one should hiccough, yawn and vent intestinal gas as often as necessary to relieve the pressure.

Two phenomena need clarification:

1) One has long hiccoughs and long yawns as if one has a serious stomach disease;

2) One defecates for as long as ten to fifteen days as if one has a serious diarrhea.

Long-term hiccoughs and long-term yawns are a symptom of stomach *ch'i* moving upward (which is analogous to prana ascending in yoga) and rushing through the esophagus. After the *ch'i* rushes up and opens the route to the esophagus, one feels refreshed in the head and chest. Further, sweet and refreshing saliva will flow continuously from the salivary glands. Taoist books describe this as a symptom of the wine of long life, a spraying of sweet dew or jade liquid and nectar. In the past, those who learned esoteric Buddhist teachings in the Hsi Kang province and Tibet payed high respect to those who emitted long hiccoughs and long yawns since these symptoms indicated that a person had attained considerable achievement in the cultivation of his *ch'i* routes.

An ordinary person who defecates frequently, whether or not he has diarrhea, could have a serious stomach disorder or a painful intestinal disorder such as colitis. Someone, on the other hand, who experiences these phenomena through the reactions of *ch'i* induced by meditation will not have pains, but will experience comfortable refreshing feelings in his head and viscera. If a person feels slightly weak, it does not matter. He might defecate a kind of purple-black sticky liquid at the end of the diarrhea-like phenomenon. This purple-black sticky liquid indicates that all the dirty deposits in the intestine and stomach are being completely eliminated. After this stage one will enter another new stage; either a mental *samadhi* state or a physiological feeling state. Still one should be careful of his diet so that he does not overeat or eat at random.

At this time, sexual intercourse should be avoided. If you have a husband or a wife, you should have intercourse as infrequently as possible. Those who cannot follow the warnings about sex and diet will have to start all over again and meditate for a long time until the diarrhea-like phenomenon happens again. Generally speaking, people frequently advance and then fail, beginning the course of meditation again and again. This is one of the key points. If one indulges in earthly desires, then, needless to say, he will not attain the goal of meditation.

Initiation of the Stomach Ch'i

The pharynx is composed of the esophagus in the back which leads to the stomach, and the trachea in the front which leads to the lungs. If someone has a disease in the tracheal system or catches a cold or the flu, coughing occurs. There are two kinds of coughs; one is a dry cough with no phlegm and one is a cough with phlegm. A dry cough is usually due to bronchitis. Some phlegm coughs are related to the diseases of the stomach which is connected with the esophagus.

A person who practices meditation after the initiation of the stomach *ch'i* and the phenomena of persistent hiccoughs and long yawns may feel something blocked in his chest that he wishes to vomit out but cannot. If he waits until he is full of ascending *ch'i*, he will suddenly vomit out dense phlegm of a turbid dark gray color. This indicates the initial opening of the *ch'i* through the esophagus. Taoists refer to this as the "twelve reiterated floors." Esoteric Buddhists calls it the throat chakra. Actually, both expressions refer to the system from the larynx down the esophagus to the stomach.

The practitioners of esoteric teachings often believe that a person will stop being troubled by illusions after his throat chakra *ch'i* route is open. This is unclear. After opening the throat chakra, one's thinking will decrease, and troubles arising from emotions and worries can be quieted. But this will not enable a person to attain "no illusions" completely, since it cannot be attained without the practice of mental *samadhi*.

Is the esophagus very important to mental and physiological health? Yes, it is extremely important. Since it is the main route of food transportation, food refuse is deposited on the walls of the esophagus. This refuse is not automatically cleaned out by physiological functions alone. Day by day deposits accumulate on the walls of the esophagus and may eventually cause many troubles, such as cancer of the esophagus. For example, if a glass is filled with milk, no matter what happens to the milk, some fine particles of milk adhere to the walls of the glass. Some yogis try to clean the esophagus and stomach by swallowing a long cloth. But, cleaning the esophagus through ascending *ch'i* is much more refined than cleaning it using this method.

The Taoist "Upper and Lower Bridges of Small Birds"

After the esophagus is opened by the ascending stomach *ch'i,* the chest feels opened and broadened. When people are in a state of extreme quiet, they may even hear crackling sounds around the heart. Then the *ch'i* entering into the lower abdomen will cause two almost spontaneous reactions: a feeling of something sinking down, and the curling up of the tongue. One of the basic meditation mudras, in Buddhism, Taoism, and the esoteric teachings of yoga, is to curl the tongue to touch the incisor gum. Generally speaking, the purpose of touching the incisor gum is to stimulate and facilitate the secretion of saliva. Part of the saliva is secreted by the pituitary gland and it effects rejuvenation. Therefore, in meditation, one can fill the mouth full of saliva by putting his tongue to the salivary gland of the incisor gums; this saliva should be swallowed often. Sometimes it even tastes slightly sweet and aromatic.

When the stomach *ch'i* ascends to pass through the esophagus, the larynx spontaneously presses downward and the tongue curls up to touch the uvula to close the larynx. At this stage one's breath, inhalation and exhalation, almost stops. This is described as harnessing the "upper bridge of small birds" and "climbing the ladder of heaven." In yoga it is called *bottled ch'i.* The phenomenon of a "condor crying at the back of the head" is perceived as clicking sounds. What is known as the "golden light appearing in front of the eyes" will become clearer and clearer. One's mind will be more quiet and be without illusions.

Special attention is required for the descending *ch'i* that is generated from the stomach to reach the lower *Tan Tien.* For a child with neither sexual knowledge nor experience who cultivates the Tao, this problem is different. For a person who has already engaged in sexual activity such as masturbation and nocturnal emissions, it is not as easy for *ch'i* to reach the *Tan Tien*. When the descending *ch'i* is passing to the lower *Tan Tien*, the nerves extending upward from the lower abdomen and pubis will register piercing pain. After this pain has subsided, in the case of men the *ch'i* will reach directly to the perineum and go through the penis, but it will only move up to the uterus in the case of women. At this moment only slight attention will bring the *ch'i* backward. The prostate gland and the perineum area will naturally contract tightly; the lower abdomen will strengthen with inner breathing which is the phenomenon of slight breathing in the lower abdomen. This is known as the "lower bridge of small birds" in Taoism.

After advancing further, the breath moving through the mouth and nose as well as the inner breath will stop completely. The genital organs and testicles of a man will retract tightly like a baby's. This initial phenomenon, known as "a retractable penis like that of the horse," is one of the thirty-two signs of a Buddha. At this stage, either overeating or going on a fast by swallowing air does not make any difference, since one has achieved the first step of *samadhi*. However, there is still a long way to go before one attains the real opening of *Tu Mai* and *Jen Mai*, true *samadhi*, and the stage beyond man and heaven.

In previous sections, we have discussed the various reaction *ch'i* causes in the *Tu Mai* and *Jen Mai*. In general, people regard these reactions as the phenomena of opening the *Tu Mai* and *Jen Mai*. This is an absurd idea. These phenomena will be helpful for health and long life if one handles them appropriately. If a person sincerely wishes to cultivate the Tao, then he should distinguish carefully between the false and the true and not regard the illusory as real.

11
Fasting and the Function of the Middle Ch'i

If the stomach *ch'i* actually ignites in one's Middle Palace and ascends *twelve floors* to pass the esophagus, one's tongue will naturally touch *the upper bridge of the small birds,* or the uvula, and the breathing place in the inner holes of the nose. The tongue will directly receive the endocrine secretions distributed by the pituitary glands, or the saliva that descends from the head. A person can swallow this sweet fragrant liquid continuously.

By and by, one will not need his nose for breathing and the coarse breath will stop naturally. This stage is sought by forcing a person to practice the *bottle ch'i* of yoga and the *self-shutting breath* of Taoism. Ultimately, one will have a stronger resistance to external circumstances such as cold, heat, humidity and either eating or fasting. At this stage a person will be able to fast a long time and consequently will need less sleep. However, one needs instructions from a wise master to decrease eating and drinking in the appropriate ways so that one can eventually fast.

A kind of *samadhi* never before experienced is gradually entered, although this is still an initial step. However, wholesome nutritious food is still needed to maintain the inner force necessary to open the *ch'i* channels of the genital glands as well as the *Yin Ch'iao, Yang Ch'iao, Yin Wei* and *Yang Wei* of the eight extra meridians.

When should one stop eating temporarily and when should he begin to eat again? This all depends upon the actual situation and cannot be laid out on paper like strategies of a battle. In Taoism, this situation is called *Ho Hou,* the strength of a fire for cooking. It is likened to adjusting the strength of a fire in cooking, since it requires self-understanding and personal attention. Inflexible rules and instructions should not be adopted since it is beneficial to retain a capacity for change.

12

A Big Belly is Not Tao

When there is a slight indication that the *Jen Mai* has opened, the inner breath, or the breath around the lower *Tan Tien* area, begins to function. Most people tend to sink the *ch'i* into *Tan Tien* naturally and cause the lower abdomen to fill and become convex. They then imagine that they have achieved a state described in a poem by the famous immortal Lu Tong Ping: "With treasure in *Tan Tien* one need not seek Tao, with no mind against the phenomenal world one need not seek Zen." In fact, this is a very undesirable phenomenon.

If one continues to concentrate on *Tan Tien*, it will cause adverse effects on the kidneys, genital glands, and the large and small intestines, and one cannot open *Tai Mai* or the *ch'i* route around the waist with ease. At this stage one should attend to contracting or shrinking the lower abdomen from the pubis to the navel and force the *ch'i* to open the *Tai Mai* area. But, one should not pay so much attention to this that he becomes bound by these feelings.

After a long while, *ch'i* will be generated from the perineum, following the meridians and veins in both legs and feet. The *ch'i* will move down step by step until it reaches the soles of the feet and gradually removes any feelings of soreness, aching, throbbing, swelling, numbness and itching. Warm, soft, light feelings of no pressure or nothingness and *happiness orgasm* will occur in every nerve and perhaps in every cell of the legs and feet. At this stage, one is happy to cross his legs and meditate for a long time to indulge in this wonderful ecstacy.

After meditating for a long time in this stage, the *ch'i* will again follow the route of *Tu Mai,* ascending to the waist and back, and then circulate freely among the nerve plexus of the scapula toward the palms and the fingertips. The entire body becomes so supple that it feels as if it has no bones. The *ch'i* will again circulate and ascend to the front of the head and will then descend and fill the entire body—arms, legs and feet—following a very tiny breath. A person almost feels as if his body does not exist.

As Lao Tze said, "One can work on *ch'i* to soften himself like a baby!" At this stage, one has achieved the initial opening of *Jen* and *Tu Mai*. For a healthy long life or the advanced cultivation of Tao, the importance of opening the *ch'i* routes in both legs through descending *ch'i* is no less important than opening the *Jen* and *Tu Mai*. One who has not experienced *happiness orgasm,* warmth, softness, and lightness in the legs should not suppose that he has opened the *Jen* and *Tu Mai*.

13

The Human Body and the Importance of Feet

Plant life originates from roots that penetrate deep into the ground. The shape of ginseng root is very similar to the human body with its two legs and feet. Thus, we can use this analogy to illustrate the importance of the feet.

Humans are the most spiritually endowed form of life. Unlike plants, the roots of the human body are at the apex of the head. The space above the human head is analogous to the soil or earth below plants. The legs and feet of a human are analogous to the branches and leaves of a plant.

If *ch'i* cannot reach the legs and feet in meditation practice and circulate freely through the nerve terminals of the arms and legs, then, although the trunk is not deteriorated, the body will be like a tree with wilted leaves and branches. In this case one will not be able to recover his or her vitality through meditation but will merely be awaiting death.

If the *ch'i* can flow freely in the legs and feet, one's waist will naturally straighten up and the hip muscles can be smoothly contracted and relaxed. While walking one will feel as if he is walking in the sky, or the ground will seem like a soft blanket, or perhaps one will feel as if he is treading on a sponge. If it happens that one is good at martial arts, he will feel as though his body is as light as a leaf or as if he could support his entire body on just one toe for a long time without tiring. On the other hand, one who is sick or very weak may experience similar feelings. However, though similar to those described above, these feelings are not actually of the same type at all. Be careful not to misinterpret one for the other.

This rough characterization of the reactions that occur upon opening the *Jen Mai* does not cover every detail. In fact, *Jen Mai* is much more difficult to open than *Tu Mai*.

Most books about meditation describe only the most obvious reactions of *Tu Mai,* and the minute details are omitted. Further, the authors of these books fail to describe the reactions that occur when the *Jen Mai* is opened.

In Taoism and in the Chinese medical arts, *Jen Mai* includes the autonomous nervous system and all the functions of the endocrine system and viscera. If a person can open *Jen Mai* and the *ch'i* can circulate freely, then he will be much healthier and experience good reactions in all visceral and metabolic functions. In Taoism it is said that, "When one *Mai* or *ch'i* route is open, one hundred *Mai* will open." This one *Mai* is *Jen Mai.*

14

Arguments Over the **Ch'i** Channels

In ancient times, discussions of *Jen Mai, Tu Mai,* and the eight extra meridians were shrouded in strange, ambiguous coverings. An attempt has been made to remove some of this coating created by previous explanations.

The processes and reactions of opening the *Ch'i Mai* are different for different people, depending upon sex and age and the strengths and weaknesses in the body. Further, different people will experience different feelings in this process due to differences in their intelligence and state of mind. However, the principles and processes described above are general enough to apply to just about everyone.

In addition to the *Tu Mai* and *Jen Mai* of Taoism, esoteric Buddhism and Indian yoga also emphasize the importance of *ch'i* routes. However, the latter emphasize the three Mai and four chakras or the three Mai and seven chakras, which are very different from the eight extra meridians of Taoism.

There have arisen arguments, refutations and flat-out contradictions between those who practice Taoism, esoteric Buddhism and yoga. The key point here is that these people have not thought deeply enough to comprehend all sides of the dispute. Whether a person is studying Taoism, esoteric Buddhism or yoga, he should understand that the only way to confirm these teachings is to suppose that the mind and body are tools for experimenting with these methods and proving claims of achievement. There is no other way.

Since we are employing the mind and body in practice, is it possible, because of our use of these different methods, to rearrange the positions of the viscera, nerves and skeleton into various forms? Of course not! There are not concrete facts which prove that there are actual differences between these different schools. However, the theory a person accepts tends to influence his or her concepts and feelings and produces corresponding hallucinations. If one insists that there are real differences, this is because he attends to certain feelings and emphasizes particular concepts, but this does not mean that one's mind and body can actually be arranged in various forms.

15

Ch'i Channels from Taoism and Buddhism

In Taoism, *ch'i Mai* was first discussed by Chuang Tze in the chapter of one of his books entitled, *Nourishment of Life*. In this chapter he recommends "following the *Tu Mai* as a meridian" and claims that all *ch'i* channels meet at the top of the head. Ever since, *Tu Mai* and *Jen Mai* have been believed to be important for the cultivation of meditation. Figures 15.2 through 15.9 illustrate the various channels and show how the energy courses through the body. These figures are shown on pages 66 through 72.

In addition to *Jen* and *Tu Mai* as the main *ch'i* channels, the eight extra meridians are central to the system of *ch'i* routes. However, Tibetan esoteric teachings that were derived from the ancient Indian tradition are entirely different from Taoist methods of cultivation. It is assumed that there are three *Mai* or *ch'i* channels and seven chakras in the human body; the left *Mai*, right *Mai* and middle or central *Mai*. The seven chakras mentioned by esoteric Tibetan teachings are, beginning from the bottom, the root chakra, the navel chakra, the heart chakra, the throat chakra, the brow chakra, the crown chakra, and, above the head, the sacred chakra. (See Fig. 15.1.)

The theory of *ch'i Mai* in esoteric Buddhism and yoga covers the functions of the *ch'i of five elements* and the *Buddha of five directions*, which includes ascending *ch'i*, descending *ch'i*, ventricle-central moving *ch'i*, left laterally moving *ch'i*, and right laterally moving *ch'i*.

Before the Wei and Chin dynasties, the Taoists emphasized the importance of these five elements and the *ch'i* of five colors. They employed terms such as *red sparrow* to indicate the front, *black turtle* to refer to the back, and *blue dragon* and *white tiger* to designate the left and right sides, respectively. These terms refer to the *ch'i* of five elements. Since the Sung dynasty, the

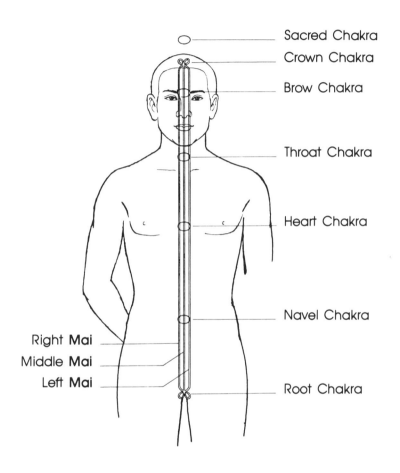

Figure 15.1
The Seven Chakras and the Three **Mai**

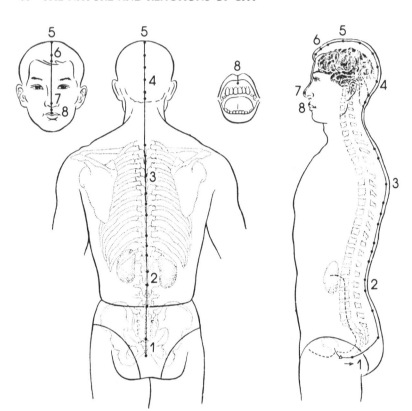

Figure 15.2
Tu Mai, The Governing Vessel

The **Tu Mai** starts in the pelvic cavity, passing through the tip of the coccyx and ascends up the middle of the spinal column (1). It moves up the back, communicating with the kidney in the lumbar region (2) and continues up the spine (3). It passes through a point that is level with the top of the ears (4) and reaches the top of the head (5). From here, it descends downward in the middle of the forehead (6), moves toward the tip of the nose (7), and ends below the septum under the upper lip (8).

The **Jen Mai** originates in the perineum (1), and moves across the pubic region (2), ascending upward along the midline of the abdomen and chest (3). It then moves upward across the sternum, rushing to a point above the throat (4). From here it ascends to a point just below the lower lip (5) and flows around the mouth (6) before terminating at a point in the center of the gums just under the upper lip (7).

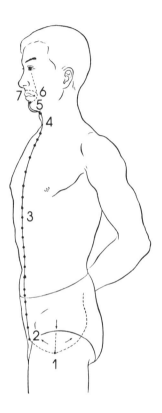

Figure 15.3
Jen Mai, The Vessel of Conception

Figure 15.4
Ch'ong Mai

This channel originates in the pelvic cavity and descends to the perineum, where it divides (1). A superficial branch ascends along the vertebral column (2). The main channel runs up the inside of the abdomen (3). It is dispersed in the chest (4), but then rushes up to meet the throat and encircle the lips (5).

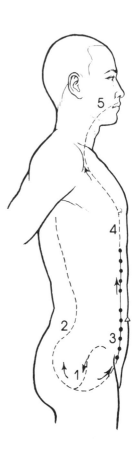

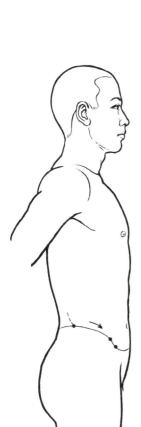

Figure 15.5
Tai Mai

This channel girds the waist at the level of the 14th vertebra in the spine, as well as the umbilicus in the front of the body. **Tai** means belt, and this channel follows a course that encircles the waist, binding up the Yin and Yang channels.

Figure 15.6
Yang Ch'iao Mai

This channel begins on the outside of the heel (1), and ascends to a point below the external malleolus of the ankle (2). It then passes along the outside edge of the fibula (3). It rushes up the side of the leg through the abdominal wall (4), ascending to the back of the shoulder (5). It zig-zags across the top of the shoulder (6), moves to the outer edge of the mouth (7), and then runs deep into the cheekbone (8). The channel continues over the dome of the head and ends at the base of the head (9).

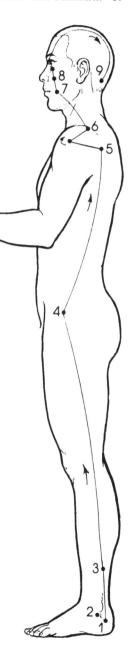

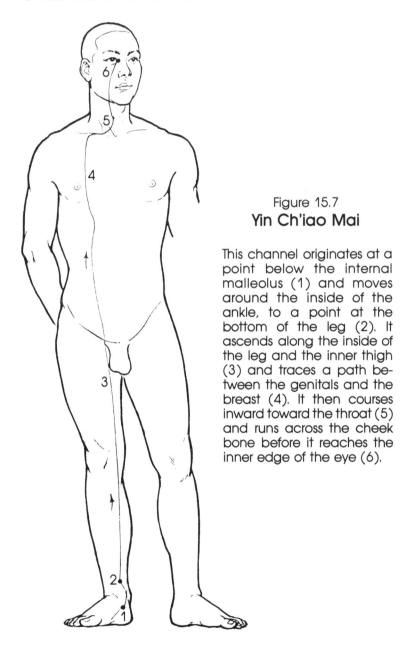

Figure 15.7
Yin Ch'iao Mai

This channel originates at a point below the internal malleolus (1) and moves around the inside of the ankle, to a point at the bottom of the leg (2). It ascends along the inside of the leg and the inner thigh (3) and traces a path between the genitals and the breast (4). It then courses inward toward the throat (5) and runs across the cheek bone before it reaches the inner edge of the eye (6).

Figure 15.8
Yang Wei Mai

This channel originates on the side of the foot below the external malleolus (1). It runs upward along the outside of the leg (2) and ascends to a point on the buttock (3). It then ascends in a path on the outside of the upper arm (4), crossing the shoulder (5) and moving up the side of the neck to the side of the head in front of the ear (6). It then descends across the forehead to a point above the eyebrow (7). From the eyebrow it turns back, moving across the top of the head, ending in the region behind the ear (8).

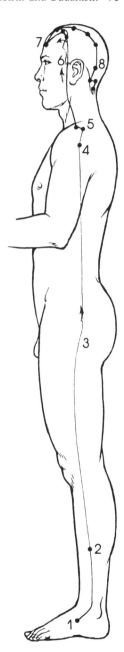

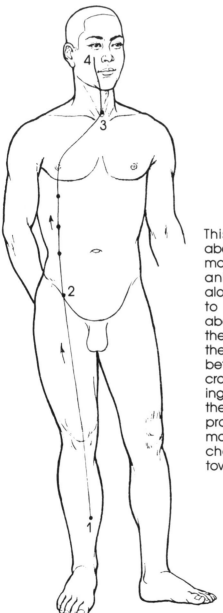

Figure 15.9
Yin Wei Mai

This channel originates about five inches above the malleolus on the inside of the ankle (1), and ascends along the inside of the thigh to a point in the lower abdomen (2). It runs along the abdomen and crosses the right half of the chest before slanting inward to cross the upper chest, moving at a diagonal to reach the edge of the laryngeal prominence (3). It finally moves across the chin and cheekbone and ascends toward the forehead (4).

Taoists have based their theories of cultivation on *Jen Mai, Tu Mai* and the eight extra meridians. They have also emphasized the importance of the functions of the left and right, or *blue dragon* and *white tiger, ch'i* channels.

If one accumulates and unites the superior views of each school through broad study, careful examination, deep thought and clear understanding, he will know that after someone actually opens the *Jen Mai* and *Tu Mai* in the course of advancement through meditation, he will naturally discover the importance of the left and right *Mai* and the middle or central *Mai.*

If one does not actually open the left and right *Mai* and the middle *Mai,* then it will be absolutely impossible for him to enter into genuine *samadhi,* or experience the condensing of *shen* and accumulation of *ch'i* and the cultivation of *ch'i* to transmute it into *shen* to enter the state of Taoism referred to as *heaven inside heaven.* In other words, after the *Jen Mai* is opened up, the left and right *Mai* of esoteric Buddhism and yoga will naturally open and, consequently, the *ch'i* can circulate without obstruction. At this stage one begins to enter the Tao and moves beyond the practice of the techniques of meditation alone. One will also begin to see some hope of opening the middle or central *Mai,* which remains.

16
What is Middle **Mai**?

The nature of the middle, or central, *Mai* is a very interesting problem. Both adherents of Taoism and esoteric Buddhism wonder whether the middle *Mai* has shape or is shapeless and whether the middle *Mai* is actually *Tu Mai* or *Jen*

Mai. Some people believe that only those who practice esoteric Buddhism actually understand middle *Mai.* They believe that the ancient Taoists did not know of the existence of the middle *Mai* and therefore think that the Taoist methods of practice are imperfect.

These arguments over the middle *Mai* were caused by a misunderstanding. It is true that Taoist books appearing during and after the Sung dynasty failed to mention the middle *Mai.* However, the *Huang Ti Nei Ching,* or the *Yellow Emperor's Classic of Internal Medicine,* and the *Huang Ting Nei Chin Ching,* or *Yellow Yard Inner View Sutra,* of ancient Taoism do include discussions of this subject.

In the *Nei Ching,* the theory of middle *Mai* (中 脈) was presented. However, it was called *Ch'ong Mai* (衝 脈). The *Huang Ting Nei Chin Ching* presupposes the importance of the central, or middle palace; it just does not emphasize the central *Mai* the way esoteric Buddhism and yoga do.

After one understands this concept and then studies the mainstream of Taoism in traditional Chinese culture, it is obvious that the *Tu Mai* and the *Jen Mai* are not considered to be the middle *Mai.* Therefore, the existence of the middle *Mai* need not be defended. The Taoist sutras and books that appeared during the Sung dynasty and thereafter seem biased and may merely represent the ideas of their authors. Therefore, they do not describe the entire spectrum of mainstream Taoism. This fact should not be misunderstood. If a person has not attained the actual state of "The middle palace *ch'i* which results in peace and harmony" and the state known as "When the middle *ch'i* is harmonized, *ch'i* is stabilized naturally and *shen* will be condensed in the right place. Beauty is within and flows to the limbs,"[9] then he will be engaged in empty talk when he claims to have opened the eight extra meridians mentioned by Taoists. Otherwise, one cannot understand the actual phenomenon of opening the middle *Mai.*

If a person opens the eight extra meridians, then he will have attained the state Chuang Tze described as, "No feelings

---

[9]This is a reference to Hexagram #2 of *I Ching.* The lines of the text are interpreted from the standpoint of meditation.

of body and limbs, no illusions, leaving form and forgetting intelligence. This is great communication (or communicating with the entire universe). This is called sitting to forget."

At this stage, the function of the middle *Mai* will be initiated. At first, it feels as if one is upwardly and downwardly communicating to infinity. A clear empty state of "no piece of clouds in ten thousand miles of blue sky" will appear naturally. Whether it is daytime or nighttime, the twinkling stars of the whole sky will appear in front of one's eyes, like one who is "observing the Amra fruit of his palm" as the Buddha is supposed to have done. In this state a person can forget all the sensations and feelings he has in ordinary times and can completely dismiss earthly concepts such as ego as well as forget arguments about who is right and who is wrong.

When one has opened the middle *Mai* it does not indicate that the whole fruit of Tao has been accomplished. Opening the middle *Mai* provides one with real security for entering the Tao. From this profound and subtle frontier one must work hard and carefully and will need the instruction of a bright master.

The left and right *Mai* will open before the middle *Mai*. Breathing exercises of yoga that aim at opening the left and right *Mai* cannot work alone. Those who actually open the left and right *Mai* will discover that their necks will be round and full. It will seem as if there is a collar encircling the neck. Without this sign one cannot claim to have opened the left and right *Mai* without engaging in empty talk.

17
Why Ch'i Channels Vibrate

The relationship between meditation and the *ch'i Mai*, the changes in *ch'i Mai*, and the physiological reactions and their phenomena have been described in previous chapters. However, the physiological reactions of the *ch'i Mai* are not always the same for everyone who practices meditation.

Why do different people with similar human bodies have various reactions? Is it because different meditation techniques and methods result in dissimilar effects and reactions in the *ch'i*? This can be explained in two ways.

First, the reactions of *ch'i* are such that it always follows *Jen* and *Tu Mai* step by step. There is no other route from the viewpoint of meditation and cultivation of Tao.

Second, there are differences in *ch'i Mai* and its physiological effects which depend upon such factors as bodily strength, health, age and sex.

Different techniques and meditation methods can produce different reactions, but this is not the major reason for dissimilar reactions in individuals and is merely a partial explanation.

Many who practice meditation experience vibrations of the body. This inner vibration often becomes an external jumping of the entire body and all its limbs, in which case a person might assume different movements and postures similar to those employed in yoga and Tai Chi Chuan. Those who are fond of mysticism may consider this to be something wonderfully mystical.

In the past some individuals specialized in the practice of divine boxing, which originated because of the occurrence of this phenomenon in meditation. Practitioners of divine boxing and people who practice "tumbling cloud," both of which were initiated from this phenomenon, often experience harmful effects and consequences.

Is this phenomenon mystical? Not at all. It is half physiological and half psychological. Even the physiological half of this reaction seems to be caused by self-suggestion. Nervous tension is often caused when a person pushes himself too hard. This tension is reflected in the subconscious mind which, in turn, causes the initial trembling of nerves and muscles. These subconscious hints subsequently enter naturally into consciousness which then enhances the vibrations and trembling. Through these subconscious self-suggestions a person often comes to shake and move his entire body and limbs in a kind of a regular pattern.

Unfortunately, ordinary people cannot always determine the reason for these vibrations and this sort of shaking. Some are afraid that they might do something wrong and so give up meditation altogether. Others believe they have already obtained divine powers or have achieved the basis of Tao and may indulge in these vibrations and movements. Further, *ch'i* cannot enter into its genuine orbits of *Jen* and *Tu Mai* due to these shaking movements of the body and so it merely circulates between the ligaments and muscles. Few people are introspective enough to discern that the cause of these movements is actually nervous tension resulting from self-suggestion.

If one intends to meditate for a healthy body and mind, or for *Nei Kung* (training the internal organs to develop uncanny strength and endurance), then it is all right to let this kind of bodily movement develop. One who does not have this aim should quiet the inner mind and relax the nerves and muscles to go "up one more floor" or lift oneself to a higher level and enter into a state of quietude.

Some people learn meditation because they suffer the pains of illnesses such as pulmonary, gastric, hepatic, renal or neuropathic diseases. It is very common for such people to feel the *ch'i* rolling in certain locations of the body during meditation. In general, those whose lungs and kidneys are deteriorating and weak often feel the *ch'i* rolling around the left and right sides of the body in certain patterns. Those who have trouble with their intestines and stomach often feel the *ch'i* circulating around the abdomen. Those who have problems in the liver or heart might feel something blocked inside the chest or diaphragm. One who breaks up this sort of blockage will suddenly feel a kind of openness or may even excrete a sticky liquid.

18

What Happens After Ch'i Channels Open?

By following the usual principles of meditation, the *Great Circulation of Heaven* and *Small Circulation of Heaven* described in Taoism will regularly occur if one can open up the *Jen* and *Tu Mai*. What about the three *ch'i* channels and seven chakras of esoteric Buddhism? What happens when they are all open and one is within the scope of the cultivation of Tao? This is a very important question. The opening of the *Jen* and *Tu Mai* and the rotation of the river chariot are believed, by the Taoists who practice to become immortals, to be the highest secret.

People often believe that the rotation of the river chariot is all-important and fail to ask the main question, which is how long should the *ch'i* be rotated. One should be aware that the rotation of the river chariot and the opening of the eight extra meridians are not the ultimate achievements in the cultivation of Tao. Strictly speaking, the rotation of the river chariot and circulation of *ch'i* in the eight extra meridians are good for health and rejuvenation, but they are merely the groundwork for the cultivation and achievement of Tao.

After the river chariot begins to rotate and *ch'i* circulates in the eight extra meridians for a certain time, at an optimum stage *ch'i* will automatically cease to rotate. The *ch'i* does not rotate because of its fullness.

The body will gradually feel light, clear, warm and soft and one will reach the state of "forgetting the body and emptiness of self." Only at this time will one suddenly introspect and recognize the roundness and illumination of the origin of nature and life. One can actually separate from and unite with the later heaven body, which has shape and form, and then combine this original nature once again with this later heaven body (or *furnace*), and mind (or *cauldron*) to continue cultivation. In this way one can either separate or unite with this body and mind and thus build a solid foundation for the cultivation of Tao. At this stage one can genuinely claim to have the *initial fruit.*

The stage and situation after the rotation of the river chariot and circulation of *ch'i* was believed to have been a mystical and heavenly secret and thus has not been mentioned in Taoist books and sutras. "The stars of the universe stop wheeling, the sun and moon are united," has been used to describe the end of *ch'i's* rotation and the clarity and emptiness of mind and body. In later ages students failed to understand the meaning of this and became confused, not knowing what to believe. It seems paradoxical that the ancients who had reached some degree of achievement wanted to help other people and, at the same time, wanted to keep everything a secret.

The separation and unification of the original nature and the body has not been explicitly described in Taoist books. At most, simple expressions such as "reenter the furnace and the cauldron" or "reorganize *Ch'ien* ($\equiv$) and *K'un* ($\equiv\equiv$)" were employed as vague images and allusions. Once again, the typical excuse was that men of achievement feared heavenly punishment upon revealing the secret. But, heaven has the virtue of helping life. Even if a person is punished by heaven for cherishing and cultivating goodness, he should still dare to help others. Otherwise, isn't a man merely selfish?

Very few can achieve genuine rotation of the river chariot and circulate *ch'i* among the eight extra meridians. Even fewer really understand the stage of separation and unification of body, mind and the origin of Nature. Therefore, even if one sincerely wants to teach this, a student with the ability to receive this supreme instruction is rare. After this stage, a person goes beyond earthly things and enters into the metaphysical realm. Even if a teacher wished to describe this in detail, a student with the wisdom and experience to receive these instructions beyond the realm of the human world would be exceptional.

19

Motives for Meditation

Most people are motivated to practice meditation for three reasons: religious emotions, mystical explorations, and long life and good health. All three of these motivations are within the realm of meditation. A person is usually influenced by the ideas of cultivating immortality described by Taoists no matter what his or her major motive may actually be.

The major tenet of Taoist immortality is that "the human body has the medicine to cure itself." In this context, medicine does not refer to material medicine alone. Material medicine is *external golden Tan* according to the theory of immortality. *Tan* indicates something a person might take to become an immortal, and it is true that external golden *Tan* might be a necessary aid to some people at certain stages of development in meditation.

Taoism, however, emphasizes the cultivation of *internal golden Tan*. I am reminded of many emperors and celebrities described in Chinese history who wanted to become immortals. A number of these people took external medicines which they believed would promote longevity but which poisoned them instead.

The *Tan Sutras*, which explore the methods for attaining immortality, merely add to the confusion since no definition of *Tan* can be found in any of them.

20

The Theory of Ching, Ch'i and Shen

During the Ming dynasty, and thereafter, the theory of transmutation of *ching* into *ch'i*, transmutation of *ch'i* into *shen*, and the transmutation of *shen* into the Void was very popular among those who practiced meditation and cultivated immortality. The phrase, "Disintegrate the empty space to enter into the state of the great golden immortal," was also popular. Therefore, most people regard *ching* within the human body as the mother of golden *Tan*. Phrases such as "keep *ching* in fullness to assure harmony" and "keep the *ching* to cultivate *ch'i*" emphasized the *transmutation of ching* as the basis for longevity and immortality. The schools of Wu Chong Hsu and Liu Hwa Yang developed their teachings from these concepts and supposed that these ideas were the basic foundation of immortality.

At the end of the Ch'ing dynasty and the beginning of the Republic of China, a Buddhist master fiercely attacked the Taoists who practiced immorality and accused them of being the children of the devil. This attack was not only unrealistic, but also went against the humble teachings of "one who swears to learn indefinite kinds of Dharma" in Buddhism. Whether one follows Taoism or Buddhism, so long as one assumes that a clean mind and little desire is the starting point, one displays good behavior according to the Vinaya school. One who attacks this assumption and supposes that it is evil, harms the great virtue of Buddhism which covers ten thousand phenomena.

Since the Ch'ing dynasty, Buddhist monks have called wet dreams the "leaking of *Tan*." They describe those who sit for a long time and never lie down as those who have "no pouring or leaking of *Tan*." The assumption is that no leaking of *ching* is the basis for *Sila*. (In Chinese, sperm is one of the meanings of *ching*, and *Sila* refers to sexual continence.) The key point is understanding real *ching* and the relationship between sperm, eggs and *ching* in connection with the transmutation of *ching* into *ch'i*.

Part III
Cultivation of **Ching, Ch'i** and **Shen**

21

Timing and Stages of Cultivation

Since the Ming dynasty, due to promotion by the Wu Liu school, the theory concerning the sequence of becoming an immortal through the cultivation of Tao has become very popular. It corresponds to the theory of the three stages of cultivation.

It is said that "Building up the foundation in one hundred days" is the preliminary stage required for transmutation of *ching* into *ch'i,* and that "pregnancy for ten months" is the preliminary stage necessary for the transmuation of *ch'i* into *shen.* "To suckle for three years" is the beginning of the transmutation of *shen* into void or emptiness. Finally, "facing the wall for nine years"[10] is the last step required for breaking up the empty space.

Some people compare this theory with the cultivation methods of esoteric Buddhism. Perhaps this is verifiable. The sequences mentioned above are similar to those experienced by

---

[10]This phrase is from the first Zen patriarch, Bodi-Dharma, who faced the wall to meditate for nine years in the Shau Lin temple.

Milorepa during his cultivation of Tao. Therefore, this sequence is deeply rooted in the hearts of the people. It can also be verified by statements derived from actual experience such as, "When *ching* is full, one does not have the desire for sex; when *ch'i* is full, one does not wish to eat; when *shen* is full, one does not want to sleep." Thus, the actual effects of the three stages of transmutation are established.

Since the Ming dynasty, eight or nine people out of ten who practice meditation or cultivate immortality always assume that working on *ching* and *ch'i* is the starting point. Some Taoist techniques that are inferior to those of the Wu Liu school also became very popular. Their followers applied a kind of pressure to acupuncture points and employed message methods to amuse their own spirits, and regarded these practices as the supreme secret required to terminate the root of sexual desires. This is a distortion indeed!

22
The Concept of **Ching**

Remarkable advances have been made in medicine which are not comparable to the self-satisfied ways of old. There are currently branches of medicine that specialize in the investigation of *ch'i,* blood and spirit. We should not ignore new knowledge and blindly adhere to an old theory, nor should we trust this new knowledge entirely and completely ignore old theories. Science advances with uncertainty. It is not like the Chinese theories of old which arrogantly claimed that a problem had been settled once and for all.

Ching in Traditional Taoist Medical Arts

Those who practice meditation for longevity and rejuvenation and those who practice ancient Chinese medical arts consider *ching*, as it occurs in the human body, to be the most essential element of life.[11] The Taoist methods for immortality suppose that *the transmutation of ching* is the main cultivation route. The forefather of Chinese medical texts, *The Yellow Emperor's Classic of Internal Medicine*, supposes that the cultivation of *ching* is the basic method for "nourishing life and longevity" and "staying away from illness and prolonging life." It says, "Two spirits roll over each other and merge to form shape. That which is born before the body is called *ching*." Further, the book states that "If one does not store up *ching* in the winter, one will be ill in the spring. If one does not store up *ching* in the summer, one will have a bowel disorder in the fall." This illustrates the importance of *ching* for nourishing life.

This concept was developed further by the Taoists in their methods for developing immortality, which emphasized renewing the brain through returning *ching* as the basic requirement for achieving longevity and rejuvenation. The ways in which one should work to renew the brain through returning *ching* and the nature of *ching* have never been clarified and there are numerous theories about this.

Ching in Modern Medical Science

Modern medical theories about ejaculation and sexual intercourse are just the opposite of Taoist theories. According to modern medical science, a normal adult should ejaculate at certain intervals of time, and it is believed to be harmful when a man suppresses his sexual behavior and tries to refrain from ejaculating.

---

[11]It is important to remember that *sperm* is one of the meanings of *ching*.

The production of sperm and eggs in the body is a natural phenomenon. It is supposed that if one believes suppressing ejaculation could possibly enhance health and add to long life, this person is suffering from illusions arising from an abnormal sexual life and strange mental states. Such claims, it is believed, are merely innocent lies.

These theories involve physiology, sexual psychology, neurology and biochemistry but, although they give numerous clues, they lack final conclusions. However, it is believed to be impossible that a pure and simple man might never ejaculate in his entire lifetime or could live a life that is healthier and longer than that of most other people. On the contrary, people who refrain from ejaculating are often melancholy due to abnormal sexual and mental states and die of cerebral apoplexy or cancer. Therefore, from the viewpoint of modern medical science, theories that advocate "renewing the brain through returning *ching* so that one can live longer" and the "transmutation of *ching* into *ch'i*" are sheer nonsense.

Side Door-Left Tao, or Heterodox Taoism

In addition to mainstream Taoist medical science, there are some schools that differ from the "clean cultivation school," which require that there be no meditation on sex. They regard renewing the brain through returning *ching* and transmuting *ching* into *ch'i* as indestructible principles. Special, though normal, techniques of sexual intercourse are required so that one can "return *ching*" to renew the brain. The phrase in the *I Ching* commentary, "One *Yin* and one *Yang* are called *Tao*" is applied here, and its meaning is often stretched to influence people through flowery language concerning meditation on sex.

During the Tang dynasty and since, there have been methods of a "living-in-fire-Taoist" for men who have wives. Tantric methods of sexual meditation in esoteric Buddhism have been popular in Tibet and Mongolia. These two methods are very similar.

Medical arts of sexual behavior secretly spread among the people. Books such as *The Yellow Emperor's Plain Woman Sutra* and *The Secrets of the Jade Bedroom,* a kind of sexual psychology, became secret. Further, some people currently teach others how to press acupuncture points to stop the leakage of semen. Those who learn these techniques often become impotent, but they are believed to have terminated the desire for sex through Tao. Some of these people get stomach problems, vomit blood, develop epistaxis, apoplexy or insanity. People who contaminate their blood by avoiding ejaculation usually become thin and their faces show a yellow cast. They may lose the joy of life but, still, such people are lucky compared to the really big disasters. Nevertheless, the claims of these Taoist books about ejaculation and leakage and methods for living in harmony with one's life force, vitality and age are compatible with the results of research done in modern medical science.

Ancient people have said, "Although it is a small Tao, it is something indeed." From the standpoint of broad study and careful thinking, a side door is also a door, and left Tao, or deflection from Tao, is also Tao. One cannot ignore or deny this completely.

Recognizing Real Ching

Are theories that advocate renewing the brain through returning *ching* and stress the transmutation of *ching* into *ch'i* just nonexistent fantasies? It is necessary to understand the concepts of the old and new Taoist teachings and medical sciences and then to return to these theories for discussion. This is the best approach.

In Taoism, primary *ching* is defined as "the original and natural vitality of life." Lao Tze's description of a baby boy provides us with the best explanation. He says, "Not to know the intercourse of male and female and yet to have an erection is the arising of *ching*." For example, when a growing baby boy is asleep, he has absolutely no consciousness of sexual desires but he may have an erection. This illustrates the distribution of the original *ching*, or vitality, and its function in growth.

Once a child has the knowledge of and need for sex, an erection can cause mental states of sexual desire and sexual desires can trigger an erection. Mind and body affect each other. Either the mind or the body initiates sexual desire. The stimulation of sexual desire produces reactions in the glands and hormones. By the mutual interaction of mind and body, endocrine secretions stimulate reactions in the testicles and uterus which, in turn, produce sperm or eggs. Sexual intercourse ends in ejaculation and orgasm.

If we understand these principles, we know that renewing the brain through returning *ching* and the transmutation of *ching* into *ch'i* should be practiced in a state of mind without the slightest sexual desire, and yet the genital organs function instinctively, as in the case of an erection. But, as long as one can keep an absolutely clean mind without sexual desire, *ching* will cool off naturally and follow the circulation of blood. One can achieve a state of returning without returning, and renewing without renewing quite naturally.

If a person ignites desire to match the activities of the genital organs, corresponding activity will be caused in the glands, hormones and semen. If one wishes to exercise control at this moment to conserve or return *ching,* turning it back by mental and physical efforts, this will add a lot of junk to the urinary tract, bladder and blood, and will affect the function of the prostate gland and increase its burden. Even worse, it could severely affect the heart, lungs, liver, nerves and brain. In Taoist sutras and books, it is advised to distinguish between the "clean and turbid origins of water." This refers to the difference between actually returning *ching* and the phenomenon described just above.

Very few, among all the people who cultivate meditation and Tao, can have an erection without experiencing the slightest desire. Someone might accidently experience the absence of desire in these circumstances but, due to the pressure on the mind arising from these physiological activities, it is very difficult to retain a clean mind.

From the standpoint of "building up foundations in one hundred days" and "transmuting *ching* into *ch'i*," it is a pity that there are as many who cultivate Tao as there are hairs on an ox but as few who achieve it as there are horns of lin.[12]

If a person lacks sexual desire because of old age, illness, impotence, or, if his sexual glands lose their ability to revive due to practice of the *side door-left Tao,* or heterodox Taoism, then this person has already brought his regenerative system of vitality to an end and unless he revives his vitality in the right way, there are no prospects for further cultivation.

We have explained *ching* and *ch'i* in terms of a physiological approach that is not at all subtle. One who wishes to proceed and trace the origins of *ching* and *ch'i* should explore the mind *ching* of Buddhism, since it may lead one to uncover the principles of real *ching* in the supreme Tan Dharma, the Dharma of immortality.

23
Transmutation of **Ching** into **Ch'i**

In order to understand the real meaning of the transmutation of *ching* into *ch'i,* we must pay attention to the connections between the phrases *Ching Shen, Ching Ch'i, Ching Force* and *Mind Force.* In traditional Chinese culture, the nouns *ching, ch'i* and *shen* were originally completely separate and independent. In later ages, *ching* and *shen* were combined to form a proper noun. It is difficult to define *Ching Shen* clearly.

---

[12]Lin is a fabulous female animal resembling the deer. *Horn of lin* describes very rare things, since lin have no horns!

During the Han dynasty and thereafter, Taoists designated *ching, ch'i* and *shen* as the major constituents of the medicine for immortality. This was based upon the *Yellow Emperor's Classic of Internal Medicine* and the *Huang Ting Ching,* or *Yellow Yard Sutra.* In the *Huang Ting Ching* it is said that "the top three medicines are *shen, ch'i* and *ching.*" This was before the importance of *ching, ch'i* and *shen* were emphasized for the cultivation of immortality. It is difficult to define *ching, ch'i* and *shen* clearly, but they can be likened to *heat, force* and *light. Ching* is the *heat* of life, *ch'i* is force and *shen* is light. If heat, force and light are missing from a human life, this is the symbol of death.

Like universal physical phenomena, *ching, ch'i* and *shen* are separate in human life but, step by step, they merge into one another. *Shen* functions in the brain; *ch'i* functions in the chest and stomach; *ching* functions in the lower abdomen, the kidneys and genital organs. The function of *ching* is closely related to the entire endocrine system in modern medical science. But, if one contemplates the view that *ch'i* must be separated from *ching,* and *shen* must be generated from *ch'i,* then one can see that this is a poor theory.

From the viewpoint of physics, heat and force are generated from light. Analogously, *ching* and *ch'i* surely arise from *shen.* In insanity, *ching* and *ch'i* have a natural tendency to be weak and feeble.

One should realize that the feeling of *happiness orgasm* is from *ching;* determination and firmness of will are from the activities of the *ch'i* force when it is full; and the agility of outstanding sharpness and wisdom arise from the quietude, or *samadhi,* of *shen.*

Buddhism emphasizes the cultivation of mind and the nourishment of nature. It promises to change a person's mental level through reflective thought. This is the starting point. The effects and attainments of Buddhists are the two kinds of *ch'i* and *shen,* similar to the supreme *Tan Dharma* or the methods employed by those wishing to become Taoist immortals. Buddhists blend the cultivation of *ching* from within.

In the Sung dynasty and thereafter, the Taoists emphasized the sequence of *transmutation of ching into ch'i,* the *transmutation of ch'i into shen,* and the *transmutation of shen into nothingness.* These methods are analogous to the three great principles of Buddhism; discipline (or observing *Sila*), cultivation of *Samadhi* (or quietude), and wisdom. A person who masters their contents will notice that there is no difference between these forms of Taoism and Buddhism.

We know that if a person insists that sperm and eggs are the basis for cultivating Tao and meditation, he should examine this problem in careful detail. However, these concepts and methods will have a different meaning for people who already have weak, deteriorated bodies or who have passed middle age and have entered old age. Cultivating Tao and meditation requires wisdom. It cannot be done from the beginning to the very end by blind belief or stubborn insistence on a biased point of view.

Human life is the combination of mind and body. The main activities of the body are *ching* and *ch'i*, which belong to the realm of feeling. The major activity of mind belongs, in a word, to the realm of perception and consciousness, *shen*.

We have covered the physiological reactions of the body, or the dynamics of the *ch'i* channels. All this belongs to the realm of feeling. Feeling is later heaven with continuous change. The initial achievement of cultivation begins with feeling and returns to feeling and perception and enters into a state of unification. There is no way to cultivate without feeling.

Everyone should understand that opening up *Jen* and *Tu Mai* and all eight extra meridians are effects of the achievements of feeling. During the course of *transmutation of ching into ch'i*, there are reactions from the fluent *ch'i* channels, and the reactions are different as the *Kung Fu*[13] advances. During the course of the *transmutation of ch'i into shen*, there are also reactions from the fluent *ch'i* channels that are different from those which occur during the *transmutation of ching into ch'i*. Since ancient times, "nine rotations form the *Tan*" has been described in the *Tan Sutra*. In later ages, some people stretched the meaning of this so that it would correspond to the reactions of the *ch'i*

---

[13]In this context *Kung Fu* does not refer to external Kung Fu, one of the martial arts, but to internal Kung Fu. *Internal Kung Fu* refers to various meditation techniques such as posture, breathing exercises, and the circulation of energy.

channels. They described how one should rotate the *ch'i* around *Jen* and *Tu Mai* to make up the number nine times nine. Although it sounds somewhat farfetched, a person could employ this idea to explain the triple cultivation of *ching, ch'i* and *shen,* which undergo inner changes step by step. One cannot denounce this.

In order to recognize the *Kung Fu* of the *transmutation of ching into ch'i,* a person should understand the nature of *real ching,* should not completely deny the function of the later heaven *ching force,* and should not incorrectly identify the later heaven sperm and eggs which are the absolute representatives of *ching.* The later heaven *ching force* is actually the manifestation of *real ching.* In other words, the source of a new life force has an absolute relationship to the thyroid, pituitary and sex glands.

When the sex glands are active and one does not experience the slightest sexual desire, at that moment he is very close to *real ching.* If this state can be retained for a time, then a force will be produced naturally which will move to the root of the nerves at the base of the spine due to the fullness in the activity of the sexual glands. This force will ascend step by step until it moves downward from the top to stimulate the regenerative function of the pituitary gland. The salivary gland will be stimulated, which will enhance the activity of the thyroid gland. The heart, mind and chest will feel joyful and open. It is difficult to describe this experience of happiness.

These initial phenomena characterize one state during the course of the transmutation of *ching* into *ch'i* along the *Tu Mai.* The achievement of Tao does not end here. For a man of practical *Kung Fu,* all the cells of his body will change and his skin will be tender and fair. This is most obvious in the cells and muscles of the face. If you look at such a man carefully, you will notice an indistinct shining on his face. On the other hand, if the cells of the facial muscles show no obvious change and a person has a reddened face, this is a kind of forked road and one should beware of the possibility of high blood pressure. This could be caused by strong attachments of the mind, the *migrations of auxiliary fire,* or it might be due to sexual desires.

The opening of *Jen Mai,* which includes opening the autonomic nervous system, may occur after the student has absorbed all the experiences we shall now describe. Fullness in the *middle palace* stomach *ch'i* will cause a sinking feeling. At this stage, if a man can clean his mind, wait quietly for spontaneous contractions of the testicles and perineum, or if a woman experiences contractions of the uterus and reactions in the breasts, he or she will feel as if there is a line of force that moves through the inside of the pubis, rushing up to the lower *Tan Tien,* and meeting the *ch'i* which descends from the *middle palace.* This will suddenly revive the activity of the *youth gland* or the abdomen, and a tremendous orgasm that exceeds sexual orgasm will occur. This orgasm will flow along the inner legs and feet and reach the soles of the feet and the toes. At this time the joy and pleasure is like that experienced by a person who drinks good vintage wine. One will feel very comfortable and easygoing. This is really the first step of achievement in the transmutation of *ching* into *ch'i.*

Depending upon sex, age, strength and weakness in the body and various natural endowments, there will be many different changes and reactions that take place for different people. At this stage of *Kung Fu,* there is a possibility that the *Kung Fu* might be lost at any moment due to some unknown something. If a person is not cautious, fails to safeguard himself or fails to develop wisdom, everything will end as if it were merely an interesting game.

The transmutation of *ching* into *ch'i* is one step of *Kung Fu* that unties the knot of the youth gland. No one should be smug and complacent about such a small achievement. These situations all belong to the realm of feeling and are, at most, evidence of the effects of processing *Kung Fu.* There is still a long way to go before reaching the Tao. Nevertheless, if one reaches this stage, rejuvenation for a long life without illness will be no problem.

24
Cultivation of **Ch'i** and Stopping the Breath

We have described the transmutation of *ching* into *ch'i* and shall now turn to the transmutation of *ch'i* into *shen*. *Ching* can be converted into *ch'i* by cultivation, but how can we transmute *ch'i* into *shen*? These ideas sound fascinating but many difficulties remain.[14]

Ching is not only semen, and *ch'i* is not merely the air we breathe. Effective cultivation consists in applying the *ch'i* of breath to trigger the *real ch'i* which is latent in the human body. It is especially difficult to define *real ch'i* for comprehension by foreign friends. In Western countries there is a tendency to correlate *ch'i* with *prana* and the kundalini. These words do not mean exactly the same thing as the *real ch'i* in the *samadhi* of Taoism. There are similarities in detail, but actually there are still differences between these concepts. The modern scientific idea of the life *energy* of the human body is somewhat closer to the meaning of *real ch'i* than the Indian concept of *prana*.

So long as various feelings occur during the course of meditation, many people tend to believe that they have already accomplished the transmutation of *ching* into *ch'i*. If these feelings spread along the spinal cord or if they occur around the chest and abdomen, a person usually believes that *ch'i* is moving along the *Tu Mai* and has already opened up the *Jen* and *Tu Mai*. So long as one is healthy or suffering only from a slight illness, he can meditate in a certain position for a long time and will experience these sensations sooner or later. But these are definitely not the genuine effects of the transmutation of *ching* into *ch'i*. These sensations are desirable effects of meditation but perhaps a person has not yet cultivated himself enough to actually build a firm foundation for the actual transmutation of *ching* into *ch'i*.

[14]Some of these difficulties will be discussed in the following chapters.

25
The Wonder and Mystery of Breath

The phenomenon of spontaneously halting the breath during meditation must be explained in order to clearly characterize the phenomena of transmuting *ching* into *ch'i*.

Chih Hsi is the spontaneous cessation of breath during meditation. In the four dhyana and the eight concentrations of Buddhist meditation, that is known as *halting the ch'i*. This is the real *Kung Fu* of *bottled ch'i* in yoga. Those who practice yoga usually practice different methods of controlling and halting the breath, but this is not the highest possible achievement. Genuine *bottle ch'i* is the spontaneous cessation of breath during meditation, what the esoteric Buddhists call *treasure bottle ch'i*.

During meditation, a person occasionally feels the cessation of his breath. When this occurs due to too much mental concentration, one feels stiff and rigid, and bodily tension gradually increases. This leads to the cessation of breath but it is not true *Chih Hsi* or a genuine case of *halting ch'i;* it is merely nervous tension. If one cannot relax and return to a natural state in such circumstances, his mind will virtually wilt and die. If this continues, he will eventually experience rigidity in every joint throughout his entire body. This is an illness. The only way one can heal oneself is to relax the mind and body as much as possible. Further, one can release the tension by exhaling slowly over and over again. It is usually a good idea to blow the air out very slowly while making the sound *Haaaaa*. This should be done repeatedly until one once again breathes normally, like a person who is sleeping. If this is done for a short time, then one will be able to advance to a higher level and go up one more floor. There are some who will remain stiff even though they are seriously attempting to relax, and they may require special instructions in esoteric Buddhism or Taoism.

A person who is actually full of the *ching* force, calm and quiet in mind and body, and has begun to enter the stage of *transmuting ching* into *ch'i* will first notice that his entire body has become soft and tender and seems to lack strength. Advancing further, one will feel as if he has no bones. The *ch'i* is filling and spreading throughout the body in the absence of the slightest feeling.

Lao Tze asked, "Can you concentrate on *ch'i* and be soft and tender like a baby?" His question characterizes this state which was also described by Mencius when he said, "The face is bright, the back (*Tu Mai*) is open and one is fluid in the limbs."

In this state a person forgets mental perceptions and physical sensations and feels as if he and the universe blend into one. The *Hung Tung* described in Taoist sutras will be experienced, and Chuang Tze's statement that there is no feeling in the body and absolutely no illusions in the mind, can be confirmed. These statements will mean more than just an empty ideal.

Attaining *Samadhi* and remaining quiet in this way, one will feel the breath moving through his nostrils becoming weaker and weaker until the breath in the lungs nearly stops. The *Tan Tien*, which is within the lower abdomen below the navel, will begin to function like the lungs. This is inner breathing, or the phenomenon of *Tai Hsi. Tai* is an embryo and *Hsi* is breath, and thus *Tai Hsi* refers to embryonic breathing or breathing like an embryo.

The esophagus and the area from the bronchia to the tip of the tongue, will be loose, fluid and comfortable when the internal organs are full of *ch'i*. At the same time, the inner breath of *Tan Tien* will become weak and come to a stop. The youth gland, which has been dormant, will recover its activity and one will be as he was as a child, without lust or passion. This will generate an incomparably strong orgasm. The testicles will contract and the *ch'i* will move up through *Jen Mai* and cause the tip of the tongue to roll up to close the uvula. When the breath ceases spontaneously in this way, the initial phenomenon of transmuting *ching* into *ch'i* has begun.

26

Changing Temperaments and Cycles of **Ch'i**

In this chapter I shall discuss the Confucian concept of *Ch'i Chih,* or changing temperaments. Changing temperaments is the most obvious achievement of those who study to seek knowledge. If people understand how to apply their knowledge to cultivation, they will become perfectly calm and treat others fairly. They will be able to deal with others and their affairs in a way that does not involve personal feelings.

This sort of cultivation begins with mental behavior and belongs to the *Kung Fu* of mental cultivation. In this context *Ch'i* indicates one's appearance or the way one seems to be, and *Chih* refers to matter or substance. When it is said that *Chih* changes, a person converts not only his mental behavior but also his physiological functions and processes. Without the physiological cultivation required to attain a state where "*Ch'i* is calm and *shen* is easy," changing temperament is merely an ideological maxim rather than practical *Kung Fu.*

The meditation techniques of the Buddhist *Tien Tai* school such as follow the breath, count the breath, observe the breath, the Taoist view that mind and body are mutually dependent, the many *Ch'i Kung* techniques, as well as some of the techniques previously described, are all very closely related to the transmutation of *ching* into *ch'i* and the transmutation of *ch'i* into *shen.*

The theories about the *ch'i* channels in the human body described in the *Tan Sutras* and meditation books are generally based upon primitive medical principles found in *The Yellow Emperor's Classic of Internal Medicine* and the *Nan Sutra.* These two books explain the movement of *ch'i* and the activities of the *ch'i* channels in abstract terms. From ancient times until the present, many who cultivate Tao and meditate are devoted to these theories inherited from the past. They believe they are perfect theories and thus often waste a great deal of their precious time and spirit by engaging in abstract, rather than practical, *Kung Fu*.

The primitive sciences of the past often employed the abstract number theories of ancient astrology and *I Ching*. Many *Tan Sutras* and Taoist books explained the functions of the *ch'i* channels in terms of the five conditions, six *ch'i*, the three hundred and sixty degrees of heaven and the sixty-four hexagrams of *I Ching*. As a consequence, people centuries later attempted to live in accordance with these ancient theories. These ancient number theories are not only vague, but may mislead modern scholars.

For example, in ancient astrology it was claimed that the round heaven is three hundred and sixty-five and one quarter degrees. The sun rotates around the earth once a day and moves one degree. One year consists of three hundred and sixty-five days and twenty-five *Ke*. On the ancient Chinese time scale, one day is one hundred *Ke*. It takes one year for the sun to circulate around the heaven. In every four years an extra day accumulates. Since the human body is a miniature of heaven and earth, the number of the movements of *ch'i* channels should also follow these rules.

According to these ancient theories, "the pulse moves three *ts'un* (about 1/10 foot) in one inhalation and three *ts'un* in one exhalation. In one breath the pulse moves six *ts'un*. In one day and night a man breathes thirteen thousand five hundred times. The pulse thus makes fifty cycles of the body." This is equivalent to saying that "during two hundred seventy breaths the pulse moves thirty-six *chang* (slightly more than ten feet) and two *ch'ih* (slightly more than one foot) in a single cycle. Fifty cycles around the body will be composed of thirteen thousand five hundred breaths, while the pulse will move about eight hundred and eleven *chang*."

Those who cultivate the Tao or meditation often practice their breathing exercises according to the principles of these theories. Actually, the clepsydra method of measuring time used by the ancients is not quite accurate. The numbers employed in these theories should be questioned and not taken for granted. According to modern medicine, the mean normal respiration rate is 18 times a minute; the mean normal pulse rate is 72 times a minute, four times the respiration rate. An average man's respiration rate adds up to 25,920 times a day— exactly the same number as the number of years in a Great Sidereal Year. A Great Sidereal Year is the length of time required for all the planets of the solar system to return to their original positions.

27

Cultivating Ch'i and Calming the Mind

If the mind and body remain in an absolutely quiet state, there will be no inward disturbance from thoughts, illusions, worries, sorrow, sadness or irritation. If there is no outward compulsion to work or exercise, a person will inhale and exhale naturally and without dizziness, sleepiness or mental chaos and confusion. After a day and a night, all one's physical energy and vitality naturally recovers its original state of fullness. This resembles the return of the planets to their positions during the Great Sidereal Cycles of the solar system.

In this state of fullness, the breath will automatically halt for a short while, indicating that breath and *ch'i* have reached the saturation point. If one can maintain this state of fullness with real calm and mental quiet, he will then arrive at the point of transmuting *ching* into *ch'i* and *ch'i* into *shen*. It is such a pity that there are so many who cultivate the Tao and meditation without knowing this principle.

Most people adhere to the old theories of the *Tan Sutra* and Taoist books; and because of their own conceited, often erroneous opinions, they often work day and night "exhaling the old and inhaling the new." They believe that they are working on the Kung Fu of transmutation. What a pity!

"Wealth and high position are just like dreams. There is no immortal who does not study."

I sincerely believe that cultivating breathing exercises and *Ch'i Kung* are not as beneficial as calming the mind. By calming the mind a person can attain a state that enables him to probe the very roots of Original Nature to effect the transformation of life.[15]

28

Three Flowers and Five **Ch'i**

What sort of *ch'i* is involved in the transmutation of *ching* into *ch'i*? In Chinese, *apoplexy* means *hit by wind*. Is the *ch'i* in the *ch'i blood* of Chinese medical science and the *wind* in apoplexy the same or different from the *ch'i* mentioned by Taoists? This is an important question.

Since the Han dynasty, the wind of the air current and the *ch'i* of human respiration have usually been believed to be the same in the Chinese medical arts. In the previous section, *ch'i* was defined as life energy, but those who meditate and cultivate longevity should not suppose that the air of the atmosphere and the *ch'i* of human respiration are the same as the *ch'i* mentioned in Taoism and esoteric Buddhism. Otherwise, one could mistake the reactions of nerves and muscles for the circulation of real *ch'i* and, consequently, would be confined to the realm of physiological sensations and feelings.

---

[15]Different breathing exercises and *Ch'i Kung* are helpful to human health, but another book would be required to discuss this in detail.

If one supposes that the only achievements attainable by cultivating *ch'i* are those pertaining to respiration and physiology, then it follows that there must be tens, or even hundreds, of methods for cultivating *ch'i* in Taoism, esoteric Buddhism and yoga. It would seem that these methods would be so similar as to differ only in detail. It cannot be denied that human respiration through the mouth, nose, skin and other organs is the basic tool for cultivation, but we should not mistakenly take this to be the essence of meditation, the nourishment of life or the Taoist *Tan Dharma*.

We should pay attention to two popular Taoist expressions in order to anticipate the phenomena that accompany the successful transmutation of *ching* into *ch'i*. They are, "three flowers assemble on the top" and "five *ch'i* go to the *Yuan*." *Three flowers* and *five ch'i* are symbolic expressions. *Ching, ch'i* and *shen* are the three flowers; the heart, liver, spleen, lungs and kidneys are the five *ch'i,* although sometimes the symbolism of the five Chinese elements—metal, wood, water, fire and earth—is employed.

In Indian yoga there are five *pranas; ascending prana, descending prana, middle moving prana, left moving prana and right moving prana.* The five *pranas* are identical to the five *ch'i* mentioned by the Taoists. On top is *Baihui,* the place at the top of the head where the upper pole of the ears meets with the sagittal suture at its midpoint. In Taoism this is known as the *Nirvana Palace,* which is related to the crown chakra and sacred chakra of esoteric Buddhism.

There are, on the other hand, many different views about the nature of *Yuan.* Some people believe that *Yuan* is the location of the *Kuan Yuan* acupuncture point, a point located several inches below the navel, which is known as *lower Tan Tien.* Other people believe that *Yuan* is *Huei Yin,* or the perineum that is called Hai *Hai Ti* (*i.e.,* the bottom of the ocean) in systems of esoteric Buddhism and yoga. Unless a real immortal appears and clarifies this matter, there is no obvious way in which we might settle this dispute and resolve the controversy. But, in Chinese philology *Yuan* is the phenomenon at the origin or the source, and this point of view can be empirically verified.

When it is said that the five *ch'i* go to *Yuan,* what is meant is that the *ch'i* of the viscera returns to its source or original position. It becomes whole, equalized, harmonized, and it is not blocked.

First, I want to explain the *three flowers assembling on the top.* A person gradually forgets his bodily feelings when the eight extra meridians are open and fluent and he has advanced in his meditation to the stage of transmuting *ching* into *ch'i.* The body both appears to exist and appears not to exist. The only feelings one experiences at this time are those resulting from reactions in the head. Quietude gives rise to the phenomenon of self-reflecting visions; that is, the eye spirit shoots inward rather than outward and one suddenly enters into a state of forgetting himself. The *Baihui (i.e.,* the top of the head) feels as if it is a high window with sun shining upon it; it is open and clear as well as incomparably cool and pleasant. It seems as if a stream of cool air has descended and permeated the entire body. This phenomenon is described in the Taoist text, *T 'i Hu Kuang Ting.*[16]

The unfortunate thing is that people often fail to understand the theory and have vague concepts. If one has the slightest illusion, a strong religious conscience, or holds to some subconscious ideology, then he could have an astral trip at this stage. Many experiences that seem to be mystical will tend to occur in combination with other illusions, but phenomena of this sort should be eradicated so that one will refrain from falling backward, and advance to higher levels.

Second, I want to explain the phenomena of *five ch'i going to Yuan:* A person will feel his breath, including the breath of the lower *Tan Tien,* suddenly halting when, or a short time after, the *three flowers have assembled on the top.* The entire body will become as soft as cotton and one will feel warm and pleasant without the respiration of later heaven. This state reminds me of those pleasant times of day when everything is calm and quiet. The mind and body, inside and outside, heaven and earth, and everything else seem to occupy their own center or to be in a neutral position; this is a state of absolute peace and harmony.

---

[16]*T'i Hu* is clarified butter and *Kuang Ting* is sprinkling water on the head in baptism.

One will not be conscious of his body or be aware of either its existence or nonexistence. Ordinary thoughts and feelings disappear without a trace.

A person who experiences this only once is like a blind cat who catches a dead mouse because he bumped into it by accident. The foundation has not yet been established. To advance from this stage to the *transmutation of ch'i into shen* the individual must go beyond the realm of meditation and become one with the Tao.

29
Meditation and Cultivation of **Shen**

On the Nature of **Shen**

To move beyond meditation to the borders of Tao, one should understand some of the concepts of *shen* employed in the Chinese medical arts, Taoism, and Tan Tao.[17]

According to the *I Ching* commentary, "*Shen* has no direction and no form. . . . That which cannot be measured by *yin* and *yang* is called *shen*."

The Yellow Emperor's Classic of Internal Medicine states: "Oh *shen*. Its sound cannot be heard with the ear. When the eye is bright and the mind is open and attentive, *shen* is revealed. It cannot be described by the mouth; only consciousness reflects all that is visible. Sometimes it shines upon the peripheral field of vision and when one relaxes one's attention, it entirely disappears. But *shen* illuminates all things and when it becomes clear it is as if the wind has blown away the clouds. It is therefore called *shen*."

[17]Tan Tao is the school of Taoism devoted to immortals and immortality.

Su Ma Chien, a famous historian of the Han dynasty, and his son, Su Ma Tan, characterized the Taoist conception of *shen*: "The first primitive force to generate human life is *shen* and life depends on form....*Shen* is the origin of life and form is its external shell....*Shen* employs *ch'i*; *ch'i* takes form....Without the intelligence and wisdom of a saint, who can grasp the *shen* of the universe and use it to create?"

The Yellow Yard Sutra, which appeared during the Han and Wei dynasties, associated *shen* with each and every organ of the human body. In each organ and cell there exists a *shen.* Given all this it should be clear that the *shen* of Tan Tao is not merely a religious concept, but is closely associated with the biological sciences as well.

Transforming Ch'i into Shen

After one attains "three flowers assembling on the top" and the "five ch'i going into yuan," he will naturally enter the phase of cultivating *shen.* Since transforming *ch'i* into *shen* is much more subtle than transforming *ching* into *ch'i,* one could be misled at this stage of meditation. The process of transforming *ch'i* into *shen* is usually accompanied by the occurrence of mental states and psychological processes that closely resemble neuroses, psychoses, and so on. Thus, the danger is that one might mistake some form of psychosis for a supernatural power and unwarranted self-congratulation for this might ultimately lead to one's own self-undoing. One should not, however, become excessively worried or frightened about this possibility. Instead, it is more important to know that the possibility exists, so as to be able to distinguish between neurotic or psychotic states and the mental powers which accompany the transformation of *ch'i* into *shen.* It should be easy to avoid the problems since one will naturally tend to develop the right sort of wisdom as he progresses in meditation.

The real wisdom of Tao is cultivated by doing good deeds and practicing virtue. Since the seeds of the wisdom of Tao cannot be planted unless one has practiced good deeds and acquired virtue, those who fail to assist others and meditate solely for selfish reasons will have attained no more than a bit of extra knowledge.

Very few actually reach this stage of transforming *ch'i* into *shen*. Buddhist books and Taoist sutras often discuss this phase of meditation by using riddles or other inscrutable statements. The idea seems to be that it is not necessary to describe it clearly, since a deity is expected to appear to instruct those who reach this level of attainment.

In order to bring the discussion of the psychological effects of meditation to a close, perhaps it will be helpful to answer some questions about what may happen during the transformation of *ch'i* into *shen*.

What indicates the beginning of the transformation of *ch'i* into *shen*? A person who actually attains the "three flowers assembling on the top" and the "five *ch'i* going into *yuan*" during meditation will undergo both psychological and physiological transformations. For example, the entire body may feel warm, like spring, and soft as a cloud. It may seem as if one's body has actually disappeared, and the person forgets himself entirely. There is no pain—only overwhelming pleasure. Mind and body, both inside and outside, are soaked in illumination. The external world shrinks and melts within, while the sphere of the inner expands in all directions and evaporates into infinite space. Consciousness and all the cosmos merge to form an indivisible unified whole. This signals the beginning of the process of the transformation of *ch'i* into *shen*.

Does the spirit actually leave the body during the transformation of *ch'i* into *shen*? The *Tan Sutras* and many Taoist books contain vivid and fanciful descriptions of the spirit leaving the body. Since the time of the Ming dynasty, the Wu and Liu schools have placed a great deal of emphasis upon methods of cultivating this phenomena. There are many descriptions of being pregnant for ten months, suckling the baby for three years, and facing the wall for nine years that have led some people to believe that successful meditation must involve astral projection. The supposition is that the spirit or divine self has a fetal body of its own which ultimately shoots out of the top of the head and ascends into heaven itself. To believe that this is a way of transforming *ch'i* into *shen* is a serious mistake.

According to the Tan Tao school, *yang shen* (or positive spirit) and *yin shen* (or negative spirit) may both account for the projection of the spirit from out of the body.

Yang shen can leave this body of flesh and blood, and yet it is a physical body with material form and a visible appearance. It can behave exactly like an ordinary human body behaves and yet it is a spiritual body with a physical form and an independent existence. It is believed to be the projection of the real spirit.

A person who says that he has an invisible and immaterial body, with or without form, that leaves and enters his physical body at will is speaking of the body of *yin shen*. *Yin shen* is similar to those bodies appearing in dreams, but it is much clearer and more distinct than ordinary "dream" bodies. Taoists maintain that the projection of *yang shen* is the ultimate achievement of meditation and the cultivation of Tao. But if one imagines that the projection of *yin shen* is the ultimate goal of Tao, then he is either an ordinary person or in the *yin* state of a spirit or a ghost.

Those who meditate and cultivate the Tao will not have any difficulty projecting *yin shen* out of the body. Some may have an experience of this sort long before reaching the stage of transforming *ch'i* into *shen*. For example, when the connection between the spirit and the body has deteriorated and grown weak, the projection of *yin shen* may occur spontaneously. This can happen to quite ordinary people who are not meditating, for it happens when one is ill, nearing death, or bordering on schizophrenia. If this can happen by itself under stressful circumstances, the student should understand that, with training, the experience will come much more easily and without the need for stress.

Sometimes people with nervous temperaments who engage in the practice of meditation may experience the projection of *yin shen*. This phenomenon is often influenced by the subconscious mind, when it is attuned to the *ch'i* ascending to the head. A person who is well versed in psychology, and who introspectively reflects upon his subconscious mind need not deceive himself about this. However, some are not infallible. A person is seldom cheated by others in life but he often fools himself with his thoughts, feelings, emotions, and actions. A person can deceive himself whether he is living an ordinary life or cultivating the Tao of immortality.

Is the cultivation of *shen* a valid process? Theoretical research, as well as firsthand experience, convinces me that the cultivation of *shen* is valid. However, in order to participate in this process, one should be completely his own master.

Merging with the cosmos is a necessary precondition for recognizing one's own spirit or divine self. This is what enables a person to advance. It enables one to condense *shen* and assemble *ch'i*; to project or refrain from projecting; to discern the size of the projected body, and to leave and return to the physical body at will. It enables one to work on the cultivation of *shen* and to achieve the Tao by means of meditation. Without perfect wisdom, virtue, harmony, and blessedness, there is no going beyond this.

Appendix I
Cultivating **Samadhi** and Wisdom Through Ch'an (Zen)

Discipline (*sila*), quietude (*samadhi*), and wisdom (*prajna*) are three aspects of *Anasrava* (*i.e.,* no leaking). These pursuits are beneficial. Quietude, or *samadhi*, is the center of discipline and wisdom. Wisdom, or *prajna*, is the foundation one uses to identify and learn the Buddha's way. To cultivate Buddhism, one must first develop *samadhi*.

A person who has attained *samadhi* will discover the solemn body of *sila*, or discipline. Wisdom will be revealed to him and he will become enlightened.

There are 84,000 ways of Dharma in Buddhism, each of which is derived from *samadhi*. *Samadhi* leads to the ocean of Bodhi. It is very important to understand that cultivation cannot be separated from *samadhi* in Buddhism.

The cultivation of *samadhi* is not merely sitting in a posture of meditation. Buddhists divide the postures of daily life into four respect-inspiring forms: sitting, standing, walking, and lying down. If one wishes to attain *samadhi*, he should meditate whenever he sits, stands, walks, or lies down. *Samadhi* can be cultivated in any of these four postures.

There are seventy-two sitting postures appropriate for the cultivation of *samadhi*, and *samadhi* is most easily attained by sitting, at least in the beginning. According to Buddhist teachings, crossing one's legs in the lotus position is the most auspicious.

One should attend to the way he sits, stands, walks, or rests, and attempt to maintain *samadhi* at all times, even when speaking or engaging in action. If one can actually accomplish this, his *samadhi* will be very strong.

After *samadhi* is developed, one will be able to identify the Bodhi. This can be accomplished as easily as picking fruit off a tree. However, one who conceives of these matters incorrectly or perceives them imprecisely will have a distorted vision of the truth.

A student can extend his knowledge by studying the sutras and practicing the cultivation of *samadhi*. The Dhyana and contemplation sutras are excellent, and books on the *Chih* and *Kuan* methods of the Tien Tai school and the sacred texts of esoteric Buddhism are highly recommended. Serious students should attempt to understand this material.

Steps Toward **Samadhi**

When beginning to cultivate *samadhi* and wisdom it is important to have determination and will power, *i.e.*, to have made a firm resolve to attain Bodhi. Second, since one's cultivation is nourished by merit, one should perform meritorious deeds and acts of charity whenever possible. By sowing the seeds of good behavior, one reaps abundant rewards. A person will succeed in entering the Tao if he has strength of will and the opportunity to exercise it in a fertile environment.

Exoteric and esoteric cultivation procedures require one to develop and embody four noble qualities, *i.e.*, boundless kindness, boundless pity, boundless joy, and limitless indifference. Strong determination and accumulated merit are the foundation of Tao. Since one is easily deflected from the truth if he lacks either one, they are the basic prerequisites of success.

The Chinese are fond of saying that a workman must have good tools if he hopes to do his work well. The situation is the same for one who practices meditation and cultivates *samadhi*. He must have good tools although he cannot acquire them in the external world. The six *indriyas,* or sense organs, provide us with excellent tools for entering into *samadhi.*

The six *indriyas* are the eye, ear, nose, tongue, body, and mind. They are confronted by six *gunas,* or sights, sounds, odors, flavors, tactile sensations, and ideas. These *mithya,* or illusions, are always coming and going. When a person mistakenly supposes these phantoms are real, he loses his original nature.

In the *Surangama Sutra,* the six *indriyas* are called the six thieves. "The eyes, ears, nose, tongue, skin and mind are the thieves. They steal our precious treasure. Living human beings are forever dragged down by these things, which explains why it is so difficult to transcend this earthly world." People who practice *samadhi* and who wish to return to their original nature can use the six *indriyas* as tools.

It is best for a person to choose one of these six tools for cultivation. He should practice using the one he chooses until he is familiar with it. He can then concentrate upon it until he reaches the first stage of *samadhi* which means he can fix his mind upon a single point with unwavering attention.

Each sense organ and each *guna* may be developed in a number of ways. A detailed explanation of this would be very complicated. Buddha said that in every thought there are 84,000 mortal distresses. It has been said, "Buddha taught all the *Dharma* (ways) because he wanted to save all minds. If I do not have all minds, why should I use all the ways?" Everyone is different. Each person should choose the way that suits him best.[18]

---

[18]Several cultivation methods will be described in the following section. If a person wants to investigate them, he should study all the exoteric and esoteric teachings. The *Surangama Sutra,* for example, describes the *dharma-paryaya* or the door to enlightenment of twenty-five Bodhisattvas.

Methods Involving Sight

First I shall discuss methods using the eye or the sense of sight. In order to cultivate *samadhi* by this method, one should find a suitable object upon which to focus his visual attention. A statue of the Buddha or something that gleams a little is best. One should concentrate on the object by fixing the gaze upon it and relaxing.

The color of the object is very important and should be carefully chosen in accordance with one's psychological and physiological condition. The appropriate color cannot be determined by a fixed rule but should be based upon one's own situation. For example, green is best for those who are extremely sensitive, red is good for people suffering from fatigue and nervous exhaustion, and blue is most beneficial for those who are unusually restless and impatient. Changing the color of the object upon which one gazes can become a handicap; it is best not to change the color of the object one uses for concentration.

If one concentrates upon illumination or light itself, one might gaze at a small lamp or candle, or else observe the light of the sun, moon, or stars. Hypnotists often make good use of the light of a crystal pendulum. It is best if the light enters the eyes from the side instead of shining directly into them. One can either gaze at the sky to observe its natural light, observe the light emitted by a fire, or look at the light reflected from a smooth body of water. However, it is usually not a good idea to gaze at one's own mirror image since this sort of concentration could trigger an out of body experience.

Buddhists, Taoists, and members of other religious schools have adopted all these methods. Students should realize that these methods are merely methods with which to get the beginner into the elementary states easily. If one clings only to these methods, one will be diverted from the real. If a person becomes preoccupied with these techniques, his mind will be confused and it may become difficult to reach the stage where the mind is steadily fixed on one point.

Phenomena of different kinds may be produced in the process of practice. Working with color and light could produce visions and phantasms as well as clairvoyance. Instruction from a good teacher may be advisable if this happens.

There are also many people who have attained enlightenment upon seeing something suddenly. Sakya Buddha, for example, became enlightened when he saw a bright star in the sky. Ling Yung, an ancient master of Zen, became enlightened when he saw a peach blossom. He wrote a poem in celebration of this, saying, "I have been looking for the guest of sword for many years. How many times have the leaves fallen and new shoots sprouted? Since I saw the peach blossom I have never again doubted." One of Ling Yung's disciples also wrote a poem describing his teacher's enlightenment: "Ling Yung saw it only once and never saw it again. Red and white twigs do not bear flowers. Fishermen on the boat came to the shore to catch fish and shrimp. This is disgusting!" Anyone who can take a similar step is obviously not limited by small methods.

Methods Involving Sound

We shall now discuss some methods involving sound. Physical sounds in the body are made chanting according to the inner method. One could chant the name of Buddha, chant sutras, or chant mantras. There are three techniques of chanting: chanting loudly, murmuring, or repeating sounds silently within the mind. When a person chants, he listens. That is, there is chanting itself, on the one hand, and listening to the resulting sound on the other. At the beginning, one may hear the continuous chanting only intermittently, but in time the sound shrinks and becomes concentrated until the mind grows quiet.

There are also methods of listening to external sounds. Any sounds may prove to be useful, although listening to flowing water, a waterfall, blowing wind, windchimes or bells, or sutras chanted in a temple, seem to produce the best effects.

The *Surangama Sutra* describes the *dharmaparyaya,* or the door through which the twenty-five Bodhisattvas passed into enlightenment. The *dharmaparyaya* of Kuan-Yin was to enter the Tao through sound, and this method is purported to be one of the very best. It is said that "The real teaching body of this place, pure and clean, is derived from listening to sound."

The mind can be settled by concentrating on sound if one can listen without growing sleepy or thinking about something else. If one continues to practice this, eventually one will suddenly enter into a very quiet realm where no sounds are heard. Then one attains the state of *samadhi* and experiences extreme quietness. This is "the tie of quietude" referred to in Buddhist sutras.

A person should not long to retain "the tie of quietude." One should realize that "the tie of quietude" is one phenomenon whereas noise is another. Both should be transcended. One should neither hope to leave the noise nor to remain in a state of quietude. It is important to realize the nonbirth of the middle way and enter into observation of wisdom.

When a person observes the nature of listening, he knows that it does not belong to either motion or quietude and is neither continuous nor interrupted.

The body is not born; there is no birth and no death for the body. Many of the ancient Zen masters did not ascend these various steps to attain enlightenment; they were enlightened upon hearing a particular sound. Therefore, those who entered the Tao by practicing Zen have always realized that Kuan-Yin's *dharmaparyaya* of listening to sound is very great indeed.

Under the direction of the master Pai Chang, a monk became enlightened upon hearing the sound of a bell. Pai Chang said, "Marvelous! This is the way of Kuan-Yin *dharmaparyaya*." Hsian Yen became enlightened while he was beating the bamboo, and Yuan Wu became enlightened when he heard the flight of mountain chicken.

The Fifth Patriarch wrote: "The wind blew from the south; the corner of the temple became a little cool." A love poem written during the Tang Dynasty says: "Frequently I call the name of the maid Sheau Yu for no reason; I merely want my lover to hear and to recognize my voice." These people became enlightened by sound. This is very great and very beautiful. Many people use the ear root *dharmaparyaya* (*i.e.*, sound), but very few understand that "the two phenomena of movement and stillness do not come into being." If a person departs from external sound and has nothing to do with it at all, he naturally attains *samadhi*. Of the two phenomena, movement and quietness, *samadhi* is the quiet phenomenon. Mind and body constitute the phenomenon of motion. If one believes that the quietude of *samadhi* is the Original Nature, then he is diverted but if he can go beyond it he enters the gate.

Methods Involving Breath

One can also attain *samadhi* by employing methods involving the breath. The Tien Tai sect and the Tibetan esoteric teachings emphasize the nose breath *dharmaparyaya*. This includes the cultivation of *ch'i* channels, *ch'i kung*, counting breath, and mind following breath. When one's breath gradually becomes more uniform and refined until it nearly stops, it is *Hsi*.

The fundamental principle of this technique is that mind and breath are closely connected. It is easiest for those who think too much or have chaotic thoughts to control the mind through the breath. If one attains *samadhi* and reflects carefully on the matter, one will discover that the mind and the breath are interdependent; each depends upon the other.

Thought is generated by breath. Breathing is manifested in thinking. When the breath is slow and even, thought is slow and quiet. Thought, breath, and quietude are not the body of Tao but functions of the power of Original Nature.

Taoists suppose that the *ch'i* of pre-heaven disperses to create *ch'i*. They imagine that when *ch'i* is gathered together it takes a particular shape or form. *Ch'i* has been taken to be the root of life and Original Nature but this is a mistake. If one identifies with something so much that he loses his own mind, he cannot understand the idea of Original Nature and its manifestations. This illustrates the difference between the right Dharma and divergent schools.

We should gain some insight into Original Nature. If a person understands that mind and breath are interdependent, then he will be free. If one supposes that mind and matter are derived from a single source, then he will understand that the methods of attaining enlightenment are merely devised for the student's convenience.

Methods Involving Bodily Sensations

Some methods of developing *samadhi* involve bodily sensation. There are two kinds of bodily *dharmaparyaya.*

In a broad sense, this includes all the techniques pertaining to six organs of sense. After all, a person uses his body when practicing these techniques. Where would the six organs of sense be without the body? All methods of cultivation require the body. In a narrow sense, the *dharmaparyaya* of the body requires concentrating on a single physical point, *i.e.,* the point between the eyebrows, the top of the head, *Tan Tien,* the sole of the foot, the coccyx, or the perineum. One might attend to the breath or use visualization techniques in order to concentrate on a single point of the body during meditation.

Sensations of cold and warmth, softness and hardness, throbbing, or aching may occur as a result of practicing these techniques. It is very easy to experience various physiological reactions, and so one could become attached to the phenomena caused by these methods. For example, although phenomena in the *ch'i* channels enable one to discern the depth of his meditation, they cause one to sink if he should become attached to the phenomena.

In the *Diamond Sutra* this sort of attachment is known as the "tenet of permanent individuality and egoism." This tenet implies that all individuals are real and have a desire for immortality. Genuine Bodhisattvas do not view things in this manner. The cultivation methods of esoteric Buddhism and Taoism could cause a person to become attached to certain phenomena since it is very difficult to free oneself from the illusion that the mind and body are real. The Zen master Huang Po often sighed about the difficulty of forgetting the self and body. In the *Perfect Enlightenment Sutra* it is said, "Men falsely suppose that the four elements are manifestations of one's own body and believe that the six sense organs and their objects are manifestations of one's own mind." People have always made this mistake. Therefore, Yung Chia, the Zen teacher, said, "Let the four elements go, do not try to catch them, just eat and drink in the quiet nature."

One might wonder how a person can rid himself of this illusion before he reaches sainthood. One can use illusion to cultivate what is real. Employing the physical body to cultivate one's Real Nature is a convenient *dharmaparyaya*. The body can be used to enter the Tao as long as one realizes that it is merely a method. One should not lose his head and identify himself with his shadow, or imagine that his shadow is real. If a person identifies with his shadow, he will sink and find it difficult to ascend. Lao Tze said, "The reason I have so much trouble is that I have a body." This is a real maxim! Ancient Zen teachers did not wish to discuss *ch'i* channels because they hoped their students would avoid attachment to them. This is a superior way of teaching.

Methods Involving Consciousness

We shall now discuss methods involving consciousness. This gate through which one can reach the Tao contains all others and it includes 84,000 methods. Consciousness is the master of the "five consciousnesses," each of which corresponds to a particular sense organ and its objects. These smaller consciousnesses are like puppets on a string. Consciousness pulls the string and the king of mind moves the puppet.

Dharma is, therefore, manufactured by consciousness. However, it seems reasonable to believe that consciousness itself should provide us with a certain method of cultivation. The methods of observing mind, *Chih* and *Kuan,* and working on

Zen are, among others, included in the dharma of consciousness itself.

A person cannot observe Original Nature or True Mind at the beginning of this work. One observes the birth and death, or appearance and disappearance, of thought. In other words, this dharma reveals the false mind of consciousness. In meditation, one should introspectively reflect upon the nature of consciousness in order to reveal the false mind of thoughts that may appear and disappear in swift succession. One should observe the origin and destruction of particular thoughts and notice where they come from and where they go. Observing a series of thoughts in this way disrupts the stream of consciousness. Former thoughts have already disappeared and can be forgotten. Subsequent thoughts have not yet appeared, and can be easily ignored. When previous thoughts have disappeared and subsequent thought has not yet appeared all is quiet. This is like a fragrant elephant crossing the river. A giant fragrant elephant plunges into the river; no matter how fast the water rushes by, the elephant ignores it and crosses the river. Its body disrupts the continuous flow of the stream. In Buddhism, this phenomenon is known as *Samatha*, or halting.

But this phenomenon is *samatha*; it is a quiet realm which is very similar to emptiness but it is not genuine emptiness. One should notice that existence comes from emptiness, and emptiness is based upon existence. Existence and emptiness are manifestations of the Original Nature, and Original Nature is the source of existence and emptiness.

At this stage, one should not care about either side but should observe the middle. Finally, one should not only ignore each of the sides but also disregard the middle. In Buddhism, this is known as observation with wisdom.

If one continues working after attaining *samatha*, one will eventually achieve *samadhi*. And, if one continues to progress after attaining observation with wisdom, then one will eventually acquire Wisdom. A person who continues to cultivate will advance step by step through the ten stages of bodhisattva development and eventually attain complete bodhi, or enlightenment. This sort of cultivation includes the teachings of the

Tien Tai sect, the treatise on the Tao torch of the bodhisattva from the yellow sect of Lamaism, meditation on the mean, or middle, and *samyagdrist* (or right views).

In the earliest period of the Chinese Zen school, no formal method was ever taught to the students. There is the saying that "A language is cut off and all behavior of the mind is extinguished." So there was no method. In a later age, students of Zen used the methods of the questioning mood or worked on *kung fu*. These all belong to the *dharma* of consciousness, although Zen techniques use consciousness in a way that is distinct from other dharmas.

What is the Zen questioning mood? It is neither the observation with wisdom nor the suspicious doubt mentioned in the discourse on *The Door to the Knowledge of Universal Phenomena*. The questioning mood penetrates deeply into the *alaya vijnana,* or the totality of consciousness, which is both relative and absolute and personal and impersonal. It is the fundamental mind-consciousness of all conscious beings, which stores and apprehends the seeds of all affairs both past and future. The mind and body were originally unified in a single totality. Before enlightenment, there may seem to be something locked within the chest that cannot escape. This tightness will break open only under the appropriate conditions, which include the right opportunity, the necessary external circumstances, and correct instructions and only when they are all combined in a single moment. It is therefore said "the divine light shining alone parts from the objects of thought, feeling, and sensation." It is also said "all these phenomena are illusory."

The last stage cannot be described in words. Attempts to describe it are: "Not until the last single sentence will it come to the solid barrier. Control the important transportation point, with no communication to the masses and the saints." This is to step upon "The Buddha of the Great Sun" and throw to "The First Buddha of the empty Kalpa" otherwise known as *Bhisma-garjita-ghosa-svara-raja.* In other words, it is "without beginning." We can hardly hope to understand this with our own thoughts since such subjects are difficult to discuss even with a thousand saints.

The Image of **Samadhi** and Wisdom

The practice of Hinayana Buddhism begins with *sila* or discipline. When a person observes *sila* he advances to *samadhi*. In *samadhi* he can acquire wisdom and attain liberation. Finally, one attains *Nirvana*.

Mahayana studies begin with alms giving, commandment-keeping, patience under provocation, zeal, and meditation, and ends with wisdom.

The *samatha* (or halting) and Buddhist contemplation induce *samadhi* and wisdom, but they are merely the beginning of cultivation.

Cultivation through the six sense organs and their objects develops into 84,000 dharmas. All of these dharmas are aimed at quieting one's thoughts. When thoughts stop, there is *samadhi*. The extent of *samadhi* differs according to what one has gained or achieved.

Some methods of cultivating *samadhi* begin with existence and apply various efforts to reach emptiness. Some begin with emptiness. In other words, empty all existence and understand absolute reality. Although there are many methods, all aim at *samadhi*.

If a person can concentrate his mind on a single object and focus his thought on one place without disturbance, then he has reached the stage of halting which is the basis for entering into *samadhi*.

The nature of *samadhi* is neither unsettled restless thinking nor dull torpor. In *samadhi* one is alert. In *samadhi* one is aware and quiet, quiet and aware. The mind is quiet but not dead quiet; it is aware. *Samadhi* resembles a fire which is nearly extinguished but retains the seed of flame in its ash. When the phenomena of awareness and quietness are conjoined there is *samadhi*.

Do not depend upon mind. Do not depend upon body. Do not depend upon nondependence. In *samadhi* thought does not dwell on mind, thought does not dwell on body, and thought does not depend on nondependence. All is dropped. This is *samadhi*.

When one begins to cultivate *samadhi,* one is usually either restless or torpid. All human beings are sometimes restless and at other times torpid. We live in these states day by day throughout the course of our lives without being aware of it.

First, I shall discuss restlessness. When a person's thought is coarse, it is easily scattered, dispersed and often chaotic. When thought is finer, it becomes somewhat more elevated.

When cultivating *samadhi,* one's mind cannot be halted at one place. A person's thinking is all mixed up. His head is full of ideas, illusions, associations of ideas, memories, and so on. These are the operations of a coarse mind.

When a person's mind becomes less coarse, it may seem that he can rest thought in a single place and yet fine thoughts still come and go like dust or gossamer. Although it is not so bothersome, there remains a kind of tender attachment occurring in the mind. This state is somewhat elevated and is referred to as *Tiao Chu.*

Most people who meditate experience this phenomenon. Some of them do not recognize tiny migratory thoughts and believe they have already attained *samadhi.* This is utterly wrong.

If one cannot stop thinking, the mind is chaotic and cannot calm down. For beginners the best plan is to physically exhaust oneself through exercise, prostrations to the Buddha, and so on. Then, one adjusts one's body until the breath grows smooth and soft and one is able to meditate again. By not paying attention to mixed thoughts, but by concentrating a single thought, one will eventually feel at ease and be able to rest his mind on just one object.

If the mind is full of mixed or confusing thoughts, treat them as you would treat guests who are forever coming and going. So long as a host neither accepts nor rejects his guests, they will eventually go away. Similarly, the mixed thoughts will gradually stop.

Whenever the mixed mind almost comes to a stop, however, one suddenly feels that he is coming to a stop. This feeling is a false thought. Whenever this false thought stops, another false thought arrives, and then it goes once again. Thus, it is very difficult to enter the realm of stopping.

If one wants to cultivate *samadhi,* it is best not to think about cultivating *samadhi.* Whenever the state of halting thought occurs, one should not focus on the idea that he is going to attain *samadhi.* This way, he can gradually enter into the state of halting the mad coursing of the mind.

During meditation one often feels that his thoughts are much more plentiful than at ordinary times. This is an indication of progress. It is like putting alum into a glass of dirty water and watching the dirt settle to the bottom. Although the water may appear to be clear, one still knows that there is dirt in it. Similarly, when a ray of sun penetrates the aperture of a door, one can see dust ranging in the air. The dirt in the water and the dust in the air exist there originally. One is usually not aware of them, but under certain conditions they are more easily detected. Although one may seem to have more thoughts during meditation, he actually has many more thoughts in the first place. They are more easily detected during meditation. Thus, this is not a problem.

If a person has too many thoughts and the power of chaotic thinking is too strong to be stopped, he can count the breaths or visualize a bright black spot either under his navel[19] or at the center of the sole of his foot in order to calm this restless mind. Another way to dela with an abundance of thought is to chant Amita Buddha: "Na-Mo-Oh-Mi-To-Fu." When a person reaches *Fu,* he should drag it out a long time, as if he were dragging his mind and body to an infinite depth.

Torpor

Now I want to discuss torpor. Coarse torpor is sleep whereas fine torpor is lethargy.

Whenever the mind or body is tired, one wants to sleep. Whenever a person needs sleep, he should not force himself to

[19]It could be harmful for women to focus their attention on the spot several fingers below the navel known as *Tan Tien.* Thus, I recommend that women only focus their attention on a bright black spot at the center of the sole of the foot. See also page 39. [The translator]

meditate. One should have sufficient sleep before beginning meditation since otherwise, he may form the habit of sleeping *during* meditation. A person who does this will never succeed.

When a person is in a state of drowsiness, his mind seems to be quiet. He neither concentrates on a single thing nor harbors coarse thoughts but he is just in the state of slumber. Although he may have no awareness of his mind or body, he is in a state of sleep rather than in a meditative state.

People who are cultivating *samadhi* can easily fall into a state of torpor. If one does not understand it and mistakes it for a kind of *samadhi,* it will result in a very pitiful failure. Sumatikirti, the founder of the Yellow sect, said that if a person mistakes this sort of torpor for *samadhi,* after his death he will reincarnate into an animal. Thus, a person should be very careful about this.

Visualization might be used in order to overcome states of torpor. For example, one could visualize a bright red point inside one's navel, and imagine it rushing upward. When this bright red point reaches the top of one's head, it will disperse. Another technique is the use of all of one's strength to shout "PEI!" Or, further, one might press his nostrils together to stop the breath until it becomes unbearable and then let the trapped air out rapidly. Finally one could take a bath in cold water or do some appropriate exercises. People who practice breathing exercises may not fall into states of torpor very easily. Torpor is often believed to be *Wang Kong,* that is, stupidity or emptiness. However, this is incorrect. *Wang Kong* refers to an idiot or simpleton who is without clarity of thought.

Lightness

When restlessness and torpor both disappear, and the mind suddenly fixes on a single thing in the absence of sleep and restlessness, then lightness occurs. For some, this sensation begins at the top of the head, whereas for others it originates in the soles of the feet.

When lightness begins at the top of the head, the top of the head feels fresh and cool as if cream were being gently poured over it. The Buddhists and Taoists call this "internal baptism." This sensation circulates around the entire body, the mind is rested, the body is relaxed, and one feels so soft and flexible that it often seems as if the bones themselves have dissolved. It is then natural for the body to become straight as a pine tree. The mind is clear and there are no feelings of restlessness or torpor in response to external surroundings. One experiences a natural state of joy. This experience of lightness, however, eventually disappears.

When lightness originates in the soles of the feet, one experiences sensations of either coolness or warmth, which move upward to the top of the head. It often feels as if this lightness moves beyond physical boundaries to penetrate the sky. The lightness that originates from the soles is much easier to retain than the lightness that originates at the top of the head. It does not disappear quite so easily.

Confucianists say that a person has the sense of spring when he has attained a state of quietude. Spring indicates feelings of warmth, growth, freshness, and joy. These feelings accompany experiences of lightness during meditation.

Lightness gradually fades when one is forced to deal with mundane affairs and cannot sustain his efforts to progress further. Thus, if it is possible, it is often best for a person who has reached this state to live alone in a quiet place.

Oftentimes one who continues to cultivate will notice that this phenomenon of lightness grows weak, but this does not mean that it actually fades away. On the contrary, if one remains in this state for a long while, the sensation of lightness will not appear to be as strong as it was at the beginning. It is very much like eating new food for the first time. In the beginning the taste is intensely fresh, but the continual eating of this same food day after day dulls the flavor and it will not appear to be nearly so refreshing as it was initially.

If one continues to maintain the state of lightness without interruption, then one's *samadhi* will become firm and stable. One will feel calm and clear. The *ch'i* channels throughout the entire body will undergo various changes, and the body will feel warm and harmonious and as if one is experiencing a strong internal orgasm. These feelings are difficult to describe but the

Chinese often say that one is "internally touched by wonderful pleasures." A person can detach himself from worldly desires only by progressing to this point.

The Top Stage

The vital force becomes highly active once one has initiated the *ch'i* currents and yang *ch'i* circulates throughout the entire body. If one forgets to focus his attention on a single phenomenon then his sexual desires will grow stronger. This could be dangerous and one should therefore be careful. Once one has passed beyond this stage, he will have already passed through the "warm" stage and advanced to the "top" stage. Then the *ch'i* and the breath will return to their origin, the mind will stop, and the external realm will grow calm and quiet.

Samadhi sila forbids the revelation of the exact nature of this state, but it is also very difficult to describe. One should know how to deal with the various changes that occur in the mind and body in order to guarantee success. *Sila,* or discipline, forbids further discussion.

A person who reaches this point in the cultivation of *samadhi* may experience the cessation of his breath and his pulse. In Buddhist, as well as in other, teachings this is described in great detail. It is wonderful listening to these descriptions although it is very difficult to attain these states. Shao Yung, for example, writes, "All thirty-six palaces are spring when coming and going to the heaven roof and the moon chamber."

Supernatural Powers

It seems appropriate to take up some discussion of supernatural powers at this point. If a person actually attains and then retains a state of *samadhi,* then he will possess the five supernatural powers: clairvoyance, clairaudience, telepathy, knowledge of the former existences of oneself and others, and the power to go anywhere or to do anything at will. Clairvoyance is the most difficult to initiate, but once it has been initiated the other four supernatural powers can be developed in succession.

Some people have a capacity to develop only one supernatural power whereas others have the ability to develop two or more of these powers simultaneously. It seems to depend upon one's natural endowments.

No matter whether one's eyes are open or closed, when clairvoyance is attained he can see clearly in all ten directions.[20] Mountains, rivers, the great earth, and fine dust particles can all be clearly observed without the slightest obstruction and appear to be seen through transparent glass. A person with clairvoyance can see whatever he wants to see as soon as he forms the intention to see it. Analogous things happen in the case of each of the other four supernatural powers.

One who engages in cultivation and develops supernatural powers before he has attained wisdom could easily be misled by incorrect thinking. He will be dragged down by this power. Such people often lose themselves and just as often lose sight of their original aims toward cultivation. Anyone who uses his power to entertain or fascinate others will surely go to the way of *Mara*.[21]

Thus, anyone who supposes that *samadhi* is the ultimate end of cultivation is like a foolish person walking down an unfamiliar road on a dark night; he could easily take the wrong turn and find himself treading through very dangerous regions. One must be vigilant and cautious since there are intersections of heresy and *Mara* scattered all along the path.

Some develop strong *samadhi* and remain so firm that they can control their mind and body completely. They may be able to stop their breath or heartbeat at will and yet, at the same

---

[20]The ten directions are the four cardinal directions (north, south, east, and west), the four intermediate directions (north-east, south-east, north-west, and south-west), the zenith (above), and the nadir (below).

[21]The way of *Mara* hinders the progress of oneself and others. It is an incorrect point of view that may arise from psychological, physiological, and external material sources.

time, they may not possess any one of the supernatural powers. Anyone who attains *samadhi*—such as many of the Brahmans and yogis of India—can perform miracles. Some of the Chinese develop and use special sword techniques. By controlling the mind and the body they are able to forge the body and the sword into a single unit. They can fly with the sword or launch the sword like a flash of light. Indeed, they often surprise and astonish the world. But, one must abandon all external things and spend many long years engaged in continuous effort in order to attain any success in these areas. Such things do not happen by chance or come about by luck.

The Annihilation of Birth and Death

Samadhi and wisdom are at the foundation of all Buddhist teachings. After attaining *samadhi*, which is the basis of all that follows, a person should give up any ideas of *samadhi* and live in a realm where "calmness and extinction appear after birth and death are annihilated." During this stage all birth and death are annihilated, even though one's body and mind no longer exist. Of course, the realm that one's body and mind have reached vanishes too, because any obtainable realm is still within the scope of birth and death. Thus, in the *Surangama Sutra,* it is written that "Although a person may attain nine degrees of *samadhi,*[22] he cannot stop the stream of transmigration to become an Arhan. This is because he clings to his false thoughts of birth and death and takes them for truth."

On the other hand, if a person abandons all thought of *samadhi* and remains in the realm of quietude and extinction, then, at this stage, the "nature void" will appear. This is the goal of Hinayana Buddhism. One releases hold of the ego and empties the self.

Anyone who cultivates the way of a Mahayana bodhisattva will eventually give up this state of emptiness. He will

[22]The nine degrees of *samadhi* consist of the four *dhyanas,* the four realms beyond form, and *samadhi* beyond thoughts and sensations.

introspect and contemplate and finally observe birth and death themselves. He will be aware of the comings and goings of all the illusory phenomena, which arise from the unborn and ascend into existence. But one should neither become attached to emptiness nor cling to existence. One should also drop the middle way and relinquish even this attachment so as to achieve universal and supernatural illumination, the two most supreme forms of enlightenment.

Anyone who possesses the fruit of universal and supernatural enlightenment understands that it is not really necessary to cultivate emptiness since he understands that all beings are originally in a state of *samadhi*. Most of the teachings of Buddha pertain to this, and further discussion does not seem to be required. If there is no *samadhi*, there is no foundation. Anyone who talks about theories of this sort without personally proving them for himself has dry wisdom and expresses empty views. He can follow the flowing stream, but he cannot move against it to return to its source. This individual cannot be his own master and all his talk is empty and false.

Many people are full of knowledge and very good at explaining principles and theories. Their speeches are so wonderful that it seems as if a lotus flower is growing on their tongues although they may not have the slightest bit of cultivation. A person who merely talks about theories and principles has "stupid stones nodding his head" in response to all the nice talk and is of no value to himself.[23] An ancient Zen master said, "It is better to act an inch than to talk a foot." A Buddhist should examine himself thoroughly and correct the mistake of saying without doing. A person should follow the sequence of the five vehicles to carry out cultivation step by step.

---

[23] The Chinese might use the expression, "he is so persuasive that even the rocks nod in agreement," to refer to a man who is a brilliant and moving speaker. When they say that a man has "stupid stones nodding his head," they are not only referring to the expression that the rocks nod in agreement, but are also suggesting that the rocks are in his head!

Appendix II
Ch'an (Zen) and Pointing at the Moon

Zen is not meditation, but it cannot be separated from meditation. Anyone who wishes to work seriously on Zen should be determined and have strong desires and firm aspirations. If a person wishes to approach the supreme *bodhi* to achieve enlightenment directly, he must realize that small virtues and accumulated merits alone cannot be counted on to produce any great success.

One cannot jump ahead and skip any important steps to enlightenment. For example, one should first work on the vehicle of a human being before proceeding to work on the vehicle of a *deva,* or heavenly being. Then one should proceed to the Mahayana, the six *paramitas* (*i.e.,* charity, purity, patience, devotion, meditation, and wisdom) and the ten thousand conducts covered in the five vehicles, perform good deeds, and cultivate virtue and *samadhi.*

It is impossible to reach the realm of *bodhi* without great sacrifice and persistent efforts. Bodhidharma said, "The Tao of Buddhas is hard and difficult. It takes aeons of effort, patience, and hard work. How can one hope to achieve Tao with few merits and little wisdom? How can one attempt to attain Tao while feeling arrogant and thinking it is easy? If one tries to do so, one tries in vain."

If a person is sincerely determined to acquire virtue, merit, and blessings when given the opportunity, he should be wise enough to choose the right way and move in a successful direction. Thus it has been said that "to learn the Tao, one must be an iron man. Iron men approach the supreme bodhi directly and ignore all right and wrong."

Further, a person must find the right teacher in order to learn the Tao. A student who sincerely seeks the Tao should follow a teacher who has experienced the Tao.

Anyone who seeks the Tao will attain the Tao. Those who fail in this lifetime can expect to succeed in a subsequent lifetime. There is no reason for anyone of unwavering faith and unrelenting effort not to succeed in attaining the Tao in three lifetimes.

An ancient master said, "Grasp one *Hua Tou* (a Zen technique) and get a strong hold on it. Then, even if one is not enlightened in this lifetime, at least one will not fall prey to any of the evil destinies at the time of one's death. Instead, one will be free to choose one's future life and can decide between the human world and a heavenly realm." Ancient masters neither deceive themselves nor mislead others. They understand the nature of the relationship between cause and effect, and we can trust what they say.

Hua Tou is like a crutch one uses when entering the Tao. A good teacher is like an old horse who knows the way. A Zen student carries a crutch and rides a good horse. The horse runs without being struck as soon as he sees the shadow of a whip. The horse breaks free of his fetters as soon as he hears the sound of the bugle.

A Zen student respects himself and respects others. He becomes enlightened under the careful guidance of a good teacher. Then he understands that he was never lost, and wonders why enlightenment is.

The questioning mood and *Hua Tou* and *Kung Fu* techniques all effect Zen, and yet these effects are not the actual dharma. To tell people that something is the dharma or that something is the truth is the same as telling a lie. To insist "I have no mind" is always foolish. To employ these methods as a yardstick designed to gauge oneself or measure others is much like changing milk into poison. It is sinful to waste one's time or lose one's life due to this.

If one despises the questioning mood, working on *Hua Tou* and *Kung Fu*, or if one believes these techniques are not real Zen dharma, then one can be compared to Lord Yeh. Lord Yeh enjoyed dragon pictures a great deal but when an actual dragon finally paid him a visit, he was absolutely terrified!

The Zen teacher Ching Yuan Wei Hsin said, "Thirty years ago, before I took up the study of Zen, I saw the mountain as the mountain and the water as the water. Later, I gained some insight by studying with a knowledgeable teacher and saw that the mountain is not a mountain and that water is not water. Now I have found a place to rest and see that the mountain is still a mountain and that water is still water. Are these observations the same or different? If anyone can elucidate this, please see me personally."

A Zen student must really work on Zen in order to attain enlightenment. Anyone who merely talks, although he may sound enlightened, is in error. An ancient master advised, "Work (on Zen) when you work and be enlightened when you are enlightened."

If one works diligently on Zen, then when one enters a stage of great death one becomes truly alive. The enlightened realm appears spontaneously. Whether in motion or at rest one cannot voluntarily possess his own mind and body because neither mind nor body actually exist.

An ancient master said that this is "like walking in the shadow of a lamp." In this state, a person sleeps without dreaming and reaches the place where being awake is the same as dreaming.

The Third Patriarch said, "If the mind is not diverse, all things are united into a single whole. If the eyes do not sleep, dreams will automatically disappear." This description is not empty talk about the dharma; it expresses the truth.

Official Lu, speaking to Zen master Nan Chuang, said, "It is wonderful! You said that the heaven, the earth, and I are from the same root. Everything is of one body." Nan Chuang replied by pointing out a peony flower in the garden whereupon he said, "I see this flower in the dream." Nan Chuang points out that the flower is an illusion and that reality is a dream. This accords with the Buddhist sutras and it conforms to the actual facts.

Anyone who attains a level where being awake is indistinguishable from dreaming should protect his achievement. One's ability to do this depends upon one's depth. The Zen master Hsueh Yen taught Tao Wu how to do this. Master Hsueh Yen told Tao Wu to wear a bamboo hat to prevent his accomplishments from seeping out, and in this way he taught his disciple how to maintain the *Kung Fu* he had attained. A similar idea was expressed by Pai Chang during a talk with Chang Ching. Pai Chang said, "It is like a cowboy carrying a stick in his hand who neither lets the cow wander into the fields nor permits her to eat the crops." If one does not guard his attainments carefully, one might lose them.

A number of Zen students who have reached the state where being awake and dreaming are indistinguishable have not attained it through diligent cultivation. Instead, they have happened upon it by chance. They are very much like the blind cat who stumbles across a dead mouse; their attainments are purely accidental and they cannot be maintained by proper controls. But, if the Zen student can guard his attainments like a cowboy protects the fields and the crops from wayward cows, then he will naturally advance to a deeper level of attainment.

When one first arrives at this stage, Zen sickness tends to occur. One may be filled with incomparable joy and yet this should be handled carefully.

As a warning to Liu Ching Cheng, the Zen master Shao Shan said, "In the future you will experience an unusual phenomenon and feel tremendous joy. If you can put a quick end to it, you will be able to become a Buddha. If you cannot control it, you may lose your mind."

As a word of caution to Ling Yuan Ching, the Zen master Huang Long Hsin said, "Those who get dharma emptiness will generally be very joyous at first. This could eventually lead to distraction and restlessness and so let them have a sound sleep."

Thus, one should focus one's attention so as not to become mentally scattered. One should guard one's accomplishments by avoiding earthly things. One should cultivate a saintly embryo until the fruit of Tao has ripened. When one realizes that all earthly appearances are indistinct from reality, then one can practice in this mundane world as well as by dwelling in the world beyond.

Once the fruit of Tao is mature, a person can always do what he says whether he is in the realm of the earth or in the realm beyond. This is the unification of enlightenment and conduct. A person who achieves this will not have any deviant views or tangential beliefs. One is willing to do whatever is required due to moral obligations or righteousness, even if one must jump into flames of fire or leap into a vat of boiling water. By refining oneself this way, one can apply one's mind freely with or without thought.

But, still, a person has not reached the end at this point. One should drop the idea that everything is illusory and leave the realm in which nothing is real. Otherwise, one will grow attached to the dharma body.

The fruit of *Nirvana* is still immature. A person must pass through several stages of birth and death in succession before he arrives at the place where mind and body are one. Eventually he will reach a point where mind can constructively dominate matter.

If a person can master all this, his mind will shine pure and bright like a full, crystal clear moon. But this still belongs to the phenomenon of initial enlightenment. We should weigh the words of Ts'ao Shan carefully, "Initial enlightenment is the same as no enlightenment."

While Nan Chuang was observing the moonlight, a monk asked him, "When did you reach the stage where your mind is like the moon?" Nan Chuang, whose last name was Wang replied, "Teacher Wang reached this stage twenty years ago." The monk then asked, "What are you doing now?" Nan Chuang ignored him and returned to his abbot room.

Why does one have to work beyond the stage of initial enlightenment? Why does one have to overcome the uphill double barrier until mind and matter are one? Perhaps these questions can be answered by citing the ancient masters.

Kuei Chong said, "The original divine light cannot be brought into full play because of the barrier created by matter and the body."

Nan Chuang said, "The wonderful function of the original ubiquitous power does not depend upon matter. The power of Tao depends upon nothing. But, the Tao must be manifested in matter since otherwise it could not be seen."

Nan Chuang also said, "Birth does not arise from the cause of birth." This suggests that one cannot create any phenomenon as a result of enlightenment.

Manjusri said, "When all is emptied it is not to create an empty phenomenon."

Chia Shan said, "There is no dharma in front of the eyes. The manas or thought and calculation are in front of the eyes. Do not become attached to the dharma in front of the eyes. Real nature cannot be reached through the eyes and the ears."

Understanding what the ancient masters said is insufficient. One should be able to put these ideas into practice. Once a person arrives at this stage, he should not remain there but should throw it aside.

In the *Dharma Words by Ling Yung*, the following is recorded:

> Ch'ang Shen asked, "From whence did life come at the beginning of the world before things were differentiated?"
> The master said, "It was like a pregnant dew pole."
> Ch'ang Shen asked, "What were things like after the world was differentiated?"
> The master said, "Like a spot of cloud in the great sky."
> Ch'ang Sheng asked, "Was the sky contaminated by that spot?"
> The master did not answer.
> Ch'ang Sheng asked further, "Why didn't life appear?"
> The master again refused to answer.
> Ch'ang Sheng then asked, "What about a pure sky without the spot?"
> The master said, "It is still flowing from real nature."
> Ch'ang Sheng asked, "What is flowing from real nature?"

The master said, "It is like a mirror which is bright and clear forever."

Ch'ang Sheng asked, "Is there anything beyond this?"

The master said, "Yes, if you break the mirror then I will see you."

Ch'ang Sheng asked, "If the mirror is broken, does that mean that one has already gone the entire way?"

The master said, "Not yet."

Ch'ang Sheng asked, "How can one accomplish it all?"

The master said, "Haven't you heard? One thousand saints will not preach at the top of the road. However, I shall describe a way for you: The very beginning is the very end. The shallowest is the deepest. Cherish goodness. Do nothing evil."

This description is theoretically correct and factually true in practice. What is dharma and what is not? Each person must choose for himself.

A person of endowment will not be deceived by other people. However, one should not talk about Zen and Tao as he pleases without first being able to practice what he preaches, or in the absence of achieving the slightest bit of cultivation. He should not think he is great if he only has intellectual understanding.

An ancient master said "great enlightenment eighteen times and small enlightenment an infinite number of times." Someone might think that this master had already forgotten body and mind, did not know anything, and entered into the state of quietness as well as great deaths and great births a number of times without reaching the highest achievement. How can we speak in such a simple way.

This problem can be explained. The big and small enlightenments discussed by the ancient master were not actually realized. They merely indicate intellectual insight. This may encourage some of the latecomers but it could also mislead some people.

Great birth and death as well as entering into *samadhi* can be experienced many times. These experiences are part of the merit of cultivation. They are also the conduct and implementation one employs after enlightenment. "He is not different from the person he was in former times but his conduct is different." This describes someone who has been enlightened. An enlightened person is the same person that he was before, although his conduct is no longer the same as it was before. Good conduct is the merit of cultivation. It is also important to remember that a person of cultivation does not become attached to the merit of cultivation, although he emphasizes it.

A highly cultivated person can directly explore the roots of origin and cut into the crux of the problem to get enlightened. He is like a thief who enters into an empty room. He comes and goes stark naked. There are no obstacles. There is nothing to be bothered or concerned about. All principles and facts that are realized are resolved. This is not a problem.

Although this may sound simple, enlightenment requires struggle and sweat. It cannot be compared to drawing eyebrows or putting makeup on to cover the surface. The word sweating should be emphasized. Some people have been enlightened without sweat, but enlightenment without hard effort is neither solid nor concrete.

Zen master Dragon Lake Pu Wun was the son of Emperor Hsi Chong, an emperor of the Tang dynasty. Although he was the crown prince of the Tang dynasty, Pu Wun was not born to wear the crown. He had, instead, divine poise, and was born to be a vegetarian. Hsi Chong tried hard to change him but failed. When Hsi Chong took refuge in Szechwan, he shaved off his hair and traveled. No one knew who he was. He visited master Su Shuang. One evening Pu Wun entered the master's room and asked, "Can you transmit the separate teaching of the Patriarch Bodhidharma to me?" The master said, "Do not slander the Patriarch." Pu Wun said, "If the separate teaching is world-renowned, how could it be false?" The master said, "Do you think it is true?" Pu Wun said, "What is your view about this?" The master said, "Wait until Mount An nods and then I shall explain it to you." Pu Wun lowered his head and said, "How marvellous!" Then he started to sweat. Later he lived at Dragon Lake and displayed many miraculous supernatural powers.

Zen master Tieh Nieu was the son of Wang from Tai Ho Pan Hsi. His ancestor Tsan of the Sung dynasty held a high political office and was in charge of all the secretarial duties in the government. Tieh Nieu was descended from Tsan in the ninth generation. Tieh Nieu was poor but honest, clean and resolute. He wished to leave the mundane world. At thirty, Tieh Nieu visited Hsi Fong and shaved off his hair. He heard the separate teaching of the Patriarch and then went to study with Hsueh Yen Ching. He stayed in the manger to engage in physical labor. One day Ching instructed the crowd: "Brothers, work hard to cultivate. If you can hold one thought without interruption for seven days and seven nights and do not get any insight, you may cut off my head and use it as a container for excrement." Tieh Nieu quietly accepted this instruction and aroused himself to work hard. He had diarrhea at the time but did not take any medicine or fluid. He held the right thought without sleeping for seven days. That midnight he suddenly felt as if the whole world was like the snow and his body could not be contained in heaven and earth. Later, he heard the sound emitted by wood hitting wood and he was enlightened. His entire body broke out into a sweat and his illness was cured. He reported to the master. The master Ching interrogated him over and over again and then ordered him to become a monk.

Wu Tsu Yen worked with Zen master Pai Yun Zuei. He asked about the talk by Nan Chuang regarding Mani jade. Pai Yun scolded him. Yen gained insight and wrote a poem, "A quiet field in front of the mountain. Clasping hands. He besought the ancestors repeatedly. Sell it and buy it back several times in order to have tender regard for pine and bamboo which attract breezes." Pai Yun approved of this poem which demonstrated some degree of enlightenment. Later Pai Yun told him: "There are several Zen persons from Mountain Lu. They all have insight. They can talk about principles. If you ask them about primary and secondary causes, they know how to answer. If you ask them to say some words on Koans, they can do that too. But they are just not right!" Yen became very skeptical and asked himself, "If a person is enlightened and can speak of his enlightenment in such a way that others can clearly understand what it is, why wouldn't he be right?" Yen worked on this question for days and suddenly got the answer. He immediately dropped everything he had ever treasured. He went to see Pai Yun. Pai Yun was so happy he waved his arms and stamped his feet for joy. Yen just smiled. Later, Yen said, "I understand the lower section of the clean wind because I once broke out into a sweat."

The stories are close to our hearts and give us the impression that we can achieve enlightenment quickly. Anyone who insists that phrases such as "great death greatly alive," "wilted tree bears flowers," "cold ashes explode the bean," and "a thunder at the top" describe the actual dharma and expects something concrete to happen will not be able to locate the Supreme Mind dharma of Zen, not even in his dreams. He will merely make those who really understand laugh. But, someone who assumes that these descriptions are only similes that have nothing to do with the facts is like an idiot talking about a dream without knowing that he is an idiot.

Does a man who becomes enlightened through Zen need to cultivate *samadhi*? One can offer a two-sided answer and say yes and no. The idea is captured by a poem: "Do not catch it, do not let it loose, leave it fully at ease; No coming, no going, moving freely." Eat rice every day but do not bite on a single grain of rice. Wear clothes everyday but do not put on a single thread. One cannot pin down anything that is materially tangible. This is a bird flying in the sky, or trying to catch the moon in a cold pond.

If a person accomplishes all this and still feels unstable, then all the dharma is like reality which one can ponder indefinitely. It does not matter. It is all right to start over again.

The Zen teacher Ling Chi wrote a poem when he was passing away: "Flowing, the stream cannot be stopped. What should one do? Infinite illumination is said to be close to it. People do not understand it. It is away from phenomena and names. As soon as a sharp sword is used, it has to be sharpened again."

Does an enlightened person need to sit in meditation? What sort of question is this? One should be able to enter into *samadhi* at any time and place by utilizing the four respect-inspiring forms of demeanor in daily life. These are walking, standing, sitting, and lying down. One should neither say that sitting in meditation is *samadhi* nor say that sitting in meditation is not *samadhi*. An enlightened person meditates naturally.

There is a short poem that says, "I stretch out my two feet to have a sleep and when I awaken heaven and earth are still the same as they were before." Is there anything that is not the same as it was previously? It is not without reason that master Huang Long Hsin called Chiu Rong a dozing tiger.

After Ling Chi was enlightened, he slept in the monks' hall. Abbot Huang Po entered the hall, saw him sleeping, and knocked the wooden wall with a crutch. Ling Chi raised his head and saw it was Huang Po and fell asleep again. Huang Po knocked against the wall again and went into another room where the head monk was sitting in meditation. Huang Po said, "The latecomer is meditating in the hall, but why are you daydreaming in here?"

After he was enlightened, Tieh Nieu was sleeping in the hall. Master Hsueh Yen Ching inspected the hall and saw him sleeping. He summoned Tieh Nieu to the abbot's room and spoke harshly, "I inspected the hall and found you were sleeping. If you can give a good reason, I'll dismiss this matter. If you do not speak out, you must leave this mountain right away." Tieh Nieu immediately answered, "The iron ox has no strength and is too lazy to till the field. So it sleeps in the snow with rope and plough. The great earth is all covered with white silver. Teh Shan, a Zen master, has no place to whip his golden whip." Ching said, "What a good iron ox!" Tieh Nieu then took this name by which we know him, which means iron ox.

Many students in the Zen group of master Su Shuang never laid down to sleep and for twenty years continued to sit in meditation. They were like the roots of a wilted tree, which prevent it from falling over. Master Su Shuang did not say that sleeping was a good idea, and he scolded his students and called them the wilted tree crowd. He also did not say that to sleep is Tao.

When master Hsuan Sa saw a dead monk, he said to the crowd, "The monk is dead but the Original Bodhi Nature is manifested everywhere. There are ten thousand miles of divine light surrounding the body. People have not understood this and have become confused." Hsuan Sa recited another poem, "There are ten thousand miles of divine light surrounding the dead body. If there is no divine light surrounding the body, where will you look? The matter is already done. One pauses. It can be seen everywhere. As soon as a person touches a point, a man of great wisdom will get the whole picture right away. If anyone misses this moment, he loses his head."

Samadhi and meditation in the Zen school are described in the Sixth Patriarch's Tan Sutra and in the annals of other Zen masters. Therefore, I shall not discuss these views further.

I shall close this book by quoting the Zen master Nan Chuang:

> It is said that the bodhisattva in the tenth stage stays in surangama samadhi where he obtains the secret dharma storage of Buddhas, and naturally obtains all kinds of samadhi, liberation and supernatural power. He can manifest his physical body in all the worlds to show that he has achieved complete and perfect knowledge, the bodhi of the Buddhas. He can rotate the great dharma wheel to enter nirvana. He can condense infinite things into a pore. He can explain one sentence from the sutra for infinite kalpas and still not exhaust its meaning. He can teach beings with different forms of life. He can cultivate the patience of no birth. In spite of all these accomplishments he will still say that he is stupid and that he knows little about the extremely fine points. How difficult it is! Be careful!

The Diamond Sutra says: "The dharma which I preach is like a raft. The dharma should be dropped. Even more so the non-dharma should be dropped."

The reader should suppose that the words in this book are just talk in a dream. If one assumes that these descriptions are real, he will turn rich clarified butter into poison. The man who talks has no mind; the person who listens is fooled.

Index